Finding & Naming Thomas Chippendale's Marquetry Team

Jack Metcalfe

To the late Tommy Limmer (Uncle Tommy),
my mentor and friend, whose skilful hands and
fervent mind underpin every page.

and

To Peter Metcalfe, my late loving brother,
whose departure on 20th January 2022 leaves a
immeasurable void in my life. His contribution to the
UK Marquetry Society and to the craft itself lives on.

Finding & Naming Thomas Chippendale's Marquetry Team

Jack Metcalfe

First published in the United Kingdom by
Jack Metcalfe
Yorkshire
England

Copyright © Jack Metcalfe 2022

The moral rights of the author have been asserted.

The author can accept no legal responsibility for any consequences arising from the application of information, advice or instructions given in this publication.

Front cover image (also p.24): Elias Martin, *Ebenisterna* (*'The ébénistes'*), 1768–1780, Nationalmuseum, Stockholm (Photo: Bodil Beckman), public domain.

Photographs of furniture which appear in this publication (unless otherwise credited) are the sole copyright © of the following: Ted Clements – Photographer; Metropolitan Museum New York; Ronald Phillips Ltd; National Trust England; Bayerische Verwaltung der staatlichen Schlösser, Gärten und Seen, Munich; J.Paul Getty Museum, Los Angeles; Chazen Museum of Art, Madison, Wisconsin; and Jack Metcalfe.

All rights reserved. No part of this publication may be reproduced, store in a retrieval system, or transmitted in any form or by any means electronic, mechanical, photocopying, recording or otherwise, without the prior written permission of the copyright owner.

Design and typesetting by Hugh Hillyard-Parker, Edinburgh, hugh@hillyard.org.uk

Contents

Chapter 1	Introduction	1
Chapter 2	**The Chippendale 'Brand'**	3
	The Influence of the *Director*	4
Chapter 3	**Chippendale's Influence on Pierre Langlois**	7
	Three Oeben tables	9
	Four Langlois Commodes	13
Chapter 4	**The Langlois 'Brand'**	19
	The Aske Hall Commode	19
	Langlois Pier Table at Temple Newsam House	21
	Langlois' Marquetry Techniques	23
Chapter 5	**Collaboration and Partnership**	26
Chapter 6	**Kitting Out a Marquetry Workshop**	29
	Dying Veneers	29
Chapter 7	**Discovering Chippendale's Marqueteurs**	31
	The 'Phillips' Commodes	31
	A Second Pair of Matching Commodes	38
	Langlois' Marquetry Style	39
Chapter 8	**Names: Finding an Inlayer and an Engraver**	41
	One Inlayer or Two?	44
Chapter 9	**Resolving Three Chippendale Marquetry Situations**	48
	1 The Harewood Library Writing Table	48
	2 The Treadle Fretsaw's Shortcoming	49
	3 Artwork Applied to the Commode Drawer Fronts	51
Chapter 10	**Lady Winn's Commode at Nostell Priory**	54
Chapter 11	**My Marquetry Education**	57
	Replica Pier Table – Book Tutorial	58
	The Replica Diana & Minerva Commode	59
	Replica Pier Table Top	60
	My Discovery of the Lunar Table	62
Chapter 12	**Bibliography**	69

ACKNOWLEDGEMENTS

The author wishes to acknowledge the following people, whose skills and expertise have in some way contributed to the writing and production of this book.

Hugh Hillyard-Parker – Editor and book designer
Ted Clements – Photographer
Dr Heinrich Piening – Furniture conservator and scientist, specialising in dye analytics, Schloss Nymphenburg, Munich
Simon Phillips – Director, Ronald Phillips Ltd, 26 Bruton Street, London
Thomas Lange – Researcher, repairer and conservator, Ronald Phillips Ltd
John Russell – Senior repairer and conservator, Ronald Phillips Ltd
Jurgen Huber – Furniture Conservator, Wallace Collection, London
Will Lawton – Proof reader
Lorraine Trickett – Proof reader
John Apps – Cabinet maker, restorer and teacher
Patrick Dingwall – Senior Director, Sothebys Auction House, UK
Simon Banks – Furniture restorer
Lawrence Mark Dundas – Owner of Aske Hall, Yorkshire
Melissa Gallimore – Freelance curator & former Curator at Harewood House
Mathew Hillyard – Archive database specialist
Daniel Prytz – Curator, Swedish National Museum, Stockholm
Leeds Museums and Galleries – Pierre Langlois's marquetry table
National Trust, Permission for displaying the commodes at Nostell Priory & The Vyne
The late Peter Thornton and William Rieder – Furniture historians
The late Elias Martin – Artist (1739–before 1818), *The Ebénistes* (painted between 1768 and 1780.)

and Neil Metcalfe – my loving son, whose scholarly knowledge guided me throughout.

CHAPTER ONE

INTRODUCTION

For many years I have been searching for the craftsman responsible for applying all the marquetry work on Chippendale's furniture. This book is the result of that research.

Thankfully, because of my many years as a practising marqueteur and as a researcher of the subject, I have been able to apply that 'insider knowledge' to this journey.

Only three years ago, I was writing under the serious assumption that Chippendale's marquetry was designed, created and applied by an independent marquetry company situated within the bustling capital city of London. Now in 2022, following much more intensive research, I have been able to uncover new information which has led to discovering that I was indeed mostly right.

Contrary to my previous assumption, this research has led not to a *company* specialising solely in marquetry work, but to an *individual* craftsman, namely Pierre Langlois, who, as you will see later in the book, produced furniture decorated with marquetry from his workshop in Tottenham Court Road, London.

I had been very fortunate during the research phase for my first book, *Chippendale's Classic Marquetry Revealed* (referred to from this point as *CCMR*), that I was allowed physical access to all twenty-one of the Chippendale marquetry productions which appear in that book.

This experience gave me detailed, first-hand insight of all the marquetry decorated furniture made by Chippendale.

Three years on, I declare my assumptions were mostly right, and that I am now able to prove why.

In order to make these ground-breaking discoveries, I have been fortunate to be able to call upon the expertise of a number of renowned artisans and specialists in this field. These talented colleagues are: Thomas Lange (researcher, furniture repairer and conservator) and John Russell (furniture repairer and conservator), who both have long experience with Ronald Phillips Ltd, Furniture Workshops and Showrooms, Mayfair, London; also, Jurgen Huber (conservator, The Wallace Collection, London); and Dr Heinrich Piening (senior conservator, Bayerische Schlösserverwaltung,

Munich), with whom I have also collaborated in researching and identifying 18th-century dyes as applied to Chippendale's marquetry using UV-VIS (ultra-violet visual) Spectrometry.

My journey has taken me along London's St Martin's Lane and Tottenham Court Road during the 1750s to 1780s, where both Chippendale and Langlois had established workshops. Behind numbers 60, 61 & 62 St Martin's Lane lay an elaborate complex of workshops, out of which Chippendale and his journeymen produced over 700 pieces of furniture and fittings during his career.

Commissions for such a vast output of work obviously didn't come out of thin air! Chippendale's masterstroke was to collect and publish a catalogue of his designs for furniture and fittings in what turned out to be a first of its kind. Entitled *The Gentleman & Cabinet Maker's Director*, Chippendale's publication was aimed not only at his 'Gentleman' customers, but also, quite explicitly, at his fellow 'Cabinet-Makers', his intention being to entice his competitors to use and emulate the classic designs held within its pages. This showed great foresight: *The Director* became, in essence, the 'Chippendale brand catalogue', a design bible from which he never deviated.

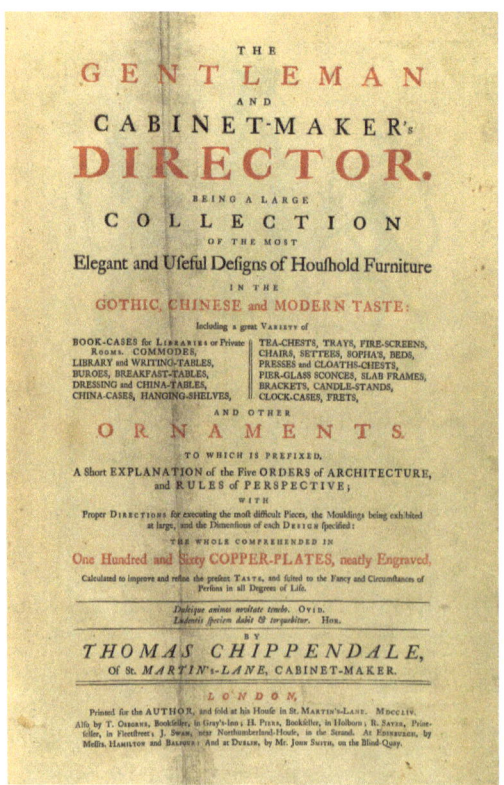

Figure 1.1 Title page of Chippendale's 'Director' (1754, 1st edition) Courtesy of the Smithsonian Libraries and Archives

CHAPTER TWO

THE CHIPPENDALE 'BRAND'

From the time of publication of the first edition of his *Director* (1754) until the mid 1770s, Chippendale enjoyed huge business and personal prestige in the field in which he worked. After 1775, his son (also called Thomas, but differentiated by the title 'the Younger') continued to run the business, also with great success.

The publication of two further editions of the *Director* (in 1755 and 1762), containing new designs alongside the established catalogue, bears witness to a flourishing business model.

Chippendale was not just a great businessman but, let us not forget, a world-class cabinetmaker, carver, turner, and designer, having spent his apprenticeship in York under master furniture-maker and carver Richard Wood.

So, what was his brand and how did it evolve?

The answer lies primarily in the detailed contents of the *Director*, and in particular in the documenting of his trademark motifs, which have become the hallmark of his artistic identity.

These classic motifs are many and include: acanthus leaves, laurel leaves, vases, urns, female figures, goats' heads, rams' heads, satyr masks, griffins, sphinxes, berries, ribbons, scrolls, swags, bellflowers, guilloches, sconces, Greek keys and, not least, the highly expressive anthemion (honeysuckle).

All of these motifs appear in both carved wood and marquetry form on Chippendale's furniture. However, one motif appearing in the final edition of the *Director* (1762), which was never carved but was to become iconic, was the sandshaded, 3D-effect 'fan' motif.

In Figure 2.1 on page 4, we see two designs for chamber organs displaying impressive front pipes, each shaded down one edge to give the all-important 3D effect. In addition, the organ on the left shows a decorative stylised oval fan above the console; this was to become one of Chippendale's best-known and most recognisable motifs, used in many forms across all his marquetry work.

Figure 2.1 Designs for chamber organs from the 3rd edition of Chippendale's 'Director' (1762), showing stylised organ pipes, hinting at the marquetry fans that were to follow.

THE INFLUENCE OF THE 'DIRECTOR'

Chippendale deliberately encouraged his competitors to use his designs and motifs through the publication of the *Director*. One competitor, whose workshops were only a few streets away at 39 Tottenham Court Road, was Pierre Langlois.

Figures 2.2 to 2.7 illustrate motifs found in Chippendale's 1st Edition of the *Director* (1754) which are found repeated in the marquetry work on Pierre Langlois' furniture (from 1759 onwards).

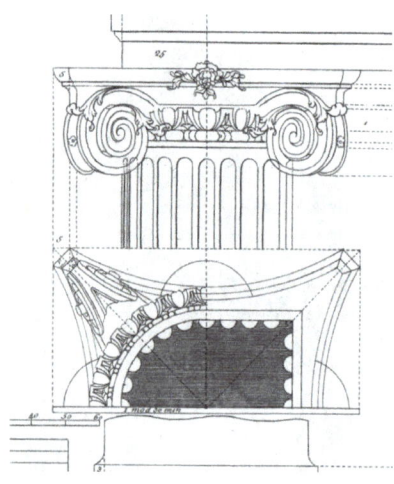

Figure 2.2 Image of half berries shown surrounding the shaded area on Plate III of the 'Director' (1st Edition), illustrating the 'Ionic Order'; these are the same half berries as used by Pierre Langlois on his marquetry commode seen in Figures 7.2 and 7.3.

2 • THE CHIPPENDALE 'BRAND'

Figure 2.3 Ribbons shown in Plate XVI of the 1st Edition were used by Pierre Langlois as marquetry motifs on his pairs of matching commodes illustrated in Figures 7.1 (on p. 32) and 7.10 (on p. 38).

Figure 2.4 Upholstery showing foliage, flowers, butterflies and birds on a pair of 'French chairs' (Plate XVIII, 1st Edition) – motifs used extensively by Langlois in his marquetry themes.

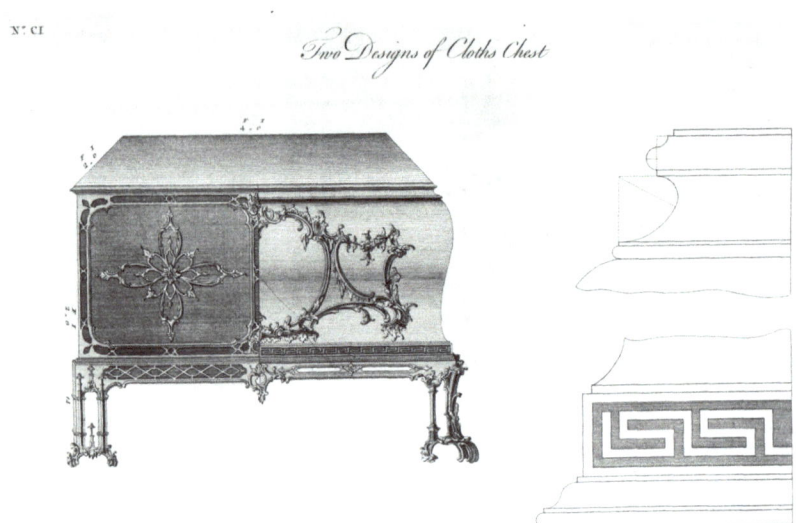

Figure 2.5 Greek key design shown as border decoration on the right-hand side of the clothes chest (Plate CI, 1st Edition) was used by Pierre Langlois on some of his bordering and banding arrangements.

Figure 2.6 (left) Sconce (candle holder) seen as it appears in the 'Director'.

In Figure 2.7 (below), it is rotated horizontally, showing how the motif, known as bellflowers, is displayed in the shapes of swags and drops. We are to see later how Langlois often used this motif in his marquetry designs. See, for example, Figures 4.4, 4.5 and 4.7 on pages 21 and 22.

CHAPTER THREE

CHIPPENDALE'S INFLUENCE ON PIERRE LANGLOIS

Pierre Langlois' past is shrouded in uncertainty. We know that Langlois was born to Daniel and Jeanne L'Anglois in London on 10th September 1718, and was baptised in the French protestant church in Soho.[1]

Although taking a French name, he was actually christened Peter, not Pierre. He is also known to have used 'Petter' (a Swedish variant of Peter), suggesting a link with fellow Swedish cabinetmakers near the London St Martin's Lane area, namely Georg Haupt and Christopher Furlohg.

Langlois set up residency at 39 Tottenham Court Road from where he produced marquetry-decorated furniture. His first recorded work was a commission for the 4th Duke of Bedford in 1759[2]. From then on his work increased in popularity, attracting both royal and titled patrons. Examples of his furniture can be seen today in the Royal Collections at both Buckingham Palace and Windsor Castle, and elsewhere.

As I have already indicated, Langlois' marquetry designs clearly echo motifs found in Chippendale's *Director*, but I now discover the possibility that Langlois received earlier training in Paris. Furniture historian Lucy Wood has suggested that Langlois may have been trained with *ébéniste* (inlayer) Jean-François Oeben, or possibly with Oeben's foreman, the Swede, Carl Petter Dahlström, in his Parisian workshop[1,3]. These connections remain speculative, as nothing concrete is known of Langlois' work before 1759.

Because of this speculative link, I decided to examine some of Oeben's marquetry, and I was intrigued to find similarities between his and Langlois' repertoires of designs.

---

[1] https://bifmo.history.ac.uk/entry/langlois-pierre-1718-1767
[2] *P. Thornton and W. Rieder published a series of five articles on Langlois in Connoisseur magazine, 1971–72, considered to be the most comprehensive record of Langlois' life and works.*
[3] *Wood, Lucy (2014) 'New light on Pierre Langlois (1718–1767)', The Furniture History Society Newsletter No. 196, November 2014, pp.1–7*

THREE TABLES BY OEBEN

1 Mechanical Toilette Table by Oeben, Paris 1754–57 (Now at the Residenz Museum, Munich)

Veneers used: rosewood, ebony, boxwood, maple/holly dyed with old fustic yellow and iron mordant to make green foliage, brazilwood, red and amaranth (aka purpleheart).

I am indebted to my dear friend and colleague Dr Heinrich Piening for bringing this piece, shown in Figures 3.1 and 3.2, to my attention.

Figure 3.2 shows a side view of the table partially open. The main table top has a brass frame edging, a feature much used by Langlois (see Figures 3.9 and 7.1). Figure 3.2 shows flowers overlapping the stringing into the border, which is similar to the way Langlois threads loops around the bordering stringers as seen at Figure 3.13. Also, the bordering stringer displays 'broken corners', which feature on many Langlois works.

Figure 3.1* Mechanical toilette table by Jean-François Oeben, c. 1754–57

* Reproduced by kind permission of the Bayerische Verwaltung der staatlichen Schlösser, Gärten und Seen, Munich

3 • Chippendale's Influence on Langlois

Figure 3.2* Mechanical toilette table by Jean-François Oeben, c. 1754–57

2 Mechanical Toilette Table by Oeben, ca. 1761–63 (Metropolitan Museum, New York)

Oak veneered with mahogany, kingwood, and tulipwood, with marquetry of mahogany, rosewood, holly, and various other woods; gilt-bronze mounts (see Figure 3.3)

Figure 3.3 Mechanical toilette table by Oeben with gilt bronze mounts on legs and edging around table top

The Metropolitan Museum gives the following description of the table on its website[4]:

> *Long recognized as one of Jean-François Oeben's masterpieces, this table (c. 1761–63) was made for his frequent and most important client, Madame de Pompadour. The main charge of her coat of arms, a tower, appears at the top of the gilt-bronze mount at each corner. The marquetry of the top (one of the finest panels in all of Oeben's furniture) was designed to reflect her interests in the arts and depicts a vase of flowers as well as trophies emblematic of architecture, painting,*

Figure 3.4 Table top showing Oeben's elaborate marquetry. The area circled is shown enlarged in Figure 3.5.

Figure 3.5 Highlighted area from Figure 3.4 showing archer's bow, arrows and torch set into a ring of daisy-type flowers. Langlois used a similar feature on a commode shown in Figure 3.13 where a torch and bow and arrows are depicted. Chippendale also displayed a similar design on his 'Lunar' table – see Figure 7.15 on page 40.

---

[4] *https://www.metmuseum.org/art/collection/search/206976*

music, and gardening. The table, completed after Oeben's death by his brother-in-law Roger Vandercruse, demonstrates Oeben's talents, not only as a creator of beautiful furniture but also as a mechanic: an elaborate mechanism allows the top to slide back at the same time as the larger drawer moves forward, thereby doubling the surface area.

3 Mechanical Toilette Table by Oeben, ca 1760 (J. Paul Getty Museum, Los Angeles)

Oak veneered with bloodwood, kingwood, amaranth, padauk, barberry, holly, boxwood, sycamore, tulipwood, hornbeam, ebony, cedar, drawer of juniper, gilt bronze mounts, brass and iron mechanism and lock, silk

Figure 3.6* Mechanical toilette table by Jean-François Oeben, c. 1754–57

* *Digital images courtesy of the Getty's Open Content Program*

A full investigation and analysis was made of this table in 2012 when Dr Heinrich Piening was commissioned to test the marquetry work using his UV-VIS Spectronomy treatment to the marquetry work top panel. This also allowed for the veneers, metals, and silk linings to be identified, as listed above. Again, note the brass edging around the top panel.

Figure 3.7* Table top as it appears now, displaying Oeben's elaborate floral marquetry.

Figure 3.8* Table top digitally recoloured to show the marquetry as it would have appeared when first made and before fading. This is a truly amazing display showing vibrant colours to both the inner display and the outer border.

* Digital images courtesy of the Getty's Open Content Program

3 • Chippendale's Influence on Langlois

In Figure 3.7, we see the marquetry as applied to the tabletop, showing elaborate floral work with the flower stems tied with a classic ribbon as replicated many times by both Langlois and Chippendale some years later in their marquetry designs.

In Figure 3.8, we see the amazing sight of the same panel showing dye colours as they would have appeared when the piece was first constructed. This is a digitally produced image applying the results of Heinrich's dye colour tests using UV-VIS Spectronomy testing. The image was constructed by Arlen Heginbotham, Conservator, Decorative Arts and Sculpture. J. Paul Getty Museum.

Having studied many more of Oeben's pieces in addition to the three works illustrated here, I can confidently state that Langlois was almost certainly trained in and influenced by Oeben's marquetry designs. Clearly, Langlois did not emulate Oeben's widely admired mechanical cabinet-making skills, as evidenced in the three toilette tables above and many more made by the master. Oeben's choice of veneers was copiously copied by his pupil as were many of his design styles displayed in the above examples.

Now let's examine a small range of Langlois' marquetry furniture productions and witness, not only Oeben's classic teachings, which possibly took place in the late 1740s to early 1750s, but also Chippendale's added influence which occurred when the 1st edition of the *Director* was published in 1754, some five years prior to Langlois' first known commission in 1759.

FOUR LANGLOIS COMMODES

Commode 1 (Metropolitan Museum, New York)

There is a clear shift in the appearance of Langlois' furniture over time. As Figures 3.9 and 3.10 illustrate, the marquetry designs draw heavily on designs in Chippendale's *Director*. This style remained constant on Langlois' marquetry. In contrast, the heavily embellished ormolu mounts on this commode were produced in the French rococo style (made by Dominique Jean, Langlois' son-in-law, who operated a metal foundry in Langlois' workshop). This style later gave way to a much less florid appearance, more in keeping with the evolving 'classic' style of the period.

As I have already suggested, Langlois' marquetry designs stem from Chippendale's *Director* (produced five years prior to Chippendale producing any marquetry himself). This is clearly why Langlois turned to the classic movement, being influenced by the wide range of artistic motifs in the *Director*.

Figure 3.9 Pierre Langlois commode, now at The Metropolitan Museum, New York, originally from Croome Court, Worcestershire (bill dated 20 July 1764, cost £55). One can see the rococo style mounts covering the legs, the design on the apron beneath the two matching doors, and on the corners and keyholes of the doors.

Note: Langlois displayed the marquetry on the two doors, plus the two outer floral arrangements (left and right) on the commode top (see Figure 3.2), as mirror images. This type of symmetry was to become a characteristic design feature he used on other commissions.

Figure 3.10 Top of the Langlois commode, displaying 'Director'-style motifs in the marquetry work, consisting of a range of tiny delicate emblems which Langlois repeatedly used throughout his career.

3 • Chippendale's Influence on Langlois

Conversely, it is thought that the influence of the French rococo style, in the design of the mounts, came through the teaching of the ébéniste (inlayer) Jean-François Oeben in his Parisian workshops (although no firm evidence exists to support this claim – nor where Dominique Jean worked prior to joining Langlois).

To illustrate his rococo versus his classic work, I have also included an examples of the latter style in this chapter (as Commode 3, on pages 16–17), showing the marked difference in style.

Interestingly, the same classic marquetry emblems were used on both Commode 1 and Commode 3, clearly telling me that whoever created the designs was initially trained by Oeben in Paris, as seen previously, then later influenced in London by Chippendale's designs found in his *Director*.

Commode 2 (Chazen Museum of Art, Madison, USA)

This is a Langlois piece of the French rococo period (see Figure 3.11). While the marquetry design is quite English in character, the ormolu mounts are typically French, being somewhat overstated and dominating the work. However, the marquetry echoes typical Langlois style, displaying flowing foliage work to both the top and the drawers. Musical instruments and sheet music feature on the top panel and the two middle drawers. This is a theme Langlois uses on later works.

Figure 3.11 Marquetry commode, attributed to Pierre Langlois, c. 1760, kingwood and various inlaid woods with ormolu mounts (Chazen Museum of Art, University of Wisconsin-Madison, USA).

Langlois also uses ormolu piping to wrap around the five drawer fronts and around the edges of the top panel – again, a feature found on some later works.

Commode 3 (Metropolitan Museum, New York)

This second commode in the Met Museum in New York, illustrated in Figure 3.12, again bears all the hallmarks of Pierre Langlois' 'classic' marquetry work, including the two outer panels displayed as mirror images. However, what has changed quite dramatically is the design of the ormolu work; this no longer echoes the heavy overbearing French rococo style of the Commode 1, but now takes on a more delicate classic appearance.

The Metropolitan Museum's attribution of this piece states the following:

Commode ca. 1771–73 British.

Formerly at St. Giles House, Dorset, this commode has been attributed to several London cabinetmakers, including Chippendale, but its maker remains unknown.

The provenance of the piece is stated as:

Anthony Ashley Cooper, 9th Earl of Shaftesbury, St. Giles House, Winborne St. Giles, Dorset (until 1955); [Frank Partridge (in 1955)].

Figure 3.12 Second Langlois ommode on display at the Metropolitan Museum New York (The top, a modern replacement, was originally veneered with pictorial marquetry.)

3 • CHIPPENDALE'S INFLUENCE ON LANGLOIS

I can sympathise with the thinking of the Metropolitan Museum; however, I believe that this work most certainly belongs to Pierre Langlois.

Although I will go on to explain my reasoning later, one small example is given here in Figure 3.13, which shows a close-up of the left door panel on this commode. It depicts archers' arrows and small foliate work suspended from a ribbon looped over the upper stringing. The ribbon is a typical feature Langlois used on many of his works, and to my mind there is no doubt as to the maker in this instance. Even though Chippendale also used ribbon designs, as we see in Chapter 7, they are markedly different to those used by Langlois.

Chapter 5 will outline further evidence for my declaration of Pierre Langlois as the maker, based on the year dates of delivery, given as ca.1771–73.

*Figure 3.13
Close-up of door panel of the second Langlois commode in the Metropolitan Museum, New York*

Commode 4 (Metropolitan Museum, New York)

This attractive yet simple piece of marquetry furniture (see Figure 3.14) I find neat, compact and very characteristic of Pierre Langlois. The commode has a pine carcass, with harewood veneer, crossbanded with rosewood, inlay of various fruitwoods.

The marquetry work is the clue to its maker. Starting with the drawers, we find bellflower swags and drops and ribbons, motifs much used by Langlois, along with daisy-type flowers, foliage and, again, ribbons on the two door panels. No image is available for the top panel. Uniquely, marquetry is not continued on the commode sides.

The fact that no metal mounts exist perhaps suggests a production made as a showpiece in Langlois' shop. The Metropolitan Museum gives a wide estimated date for the piece spanning ten years (ca. 1770–80), which is perhaps a clue to why no provenance is recorded. In Chapter 5, I explain how and when this piece could have been sold.

Figure 3.14 Third Langlois commode in the collection of the Metropolitan Museum New York

CHAPTER FOUR

THE LANGLOIS 'BRAND'

THE ASKE HALL COMMODE

My introduction to Langlois' marquetry came in 2006 at Aske Hall in North Yorkshire, although at the time I did not realise it was his marquetry work I was looking at.

I had been contacted by Patrick Dingwall (now Senior Director at Sotheby's Auction House, London, but at the time Furniture and Marquetry Conservator of Dingwall and Banks, based at Constable Burton Hall, North Yorkshire), and his business partner Simon Banks to give my opinion on a commode held at Aske Hall near Richmond. I was given permission by owner Mark Dundas to bring photographer Ted Clements with me to take photographs of the piece. We arrived on that day and were taken directly to the commode, shown in Figure 4.1.

Figure 4.1* The commode at Aske Hall

* *Reproduced by kind permission of Aske Hall*

I was asked if I had any idea what could have caused the number of black stain marks seen on the two door fronts. Various options were discussed, yet no obvious conclusion emerged from our discussions. Clearly, we all agreed the marks had appeared sometime after the commode was first delivered (c.1770), otherwise the marks would have been rectified by the maker. I since discovered some years later that fustic veneers proved to be extremely unstable, resulting in the initial colour of the wood – a vibrant yellow – turning (within two to three years) to a dirty-brown colour. This resulted in furniture makers in London abandoning the use of this wood permanently. It is now my belief that inherent rogue elements developed within fustic, which in turn manifested into black stain marks.

The owner was under the impression that the piece was made by Chippendale. However, seeing the marquetry design laid out before me caused me to question whether that was a correct assumption. I have to accept that in 2006 I was only beginning to identify Chippendale marquetry, and it was not until twelve years later after I had seen, researched and written about the full range of his works, that I was able to confidently identify the true maker of the decorative marquetry on this commode.

Chippendale Tercentenary Exhibition 2018

Following the Aske Hall visit in 2006, I fast-forward twelve years to the Chippendale Tercentenary Exhibition staged at the Leeds City Museum in 2018. Among the exhibits displayed was the Aske Hall Commode, described as the work of Chippendale the Elder by exhibition curators Adam Bowett and James Lomax (of the Chippendale Society).

There is always a problem when historically placing a piece of antique furniture, where documented evidence does not exist. Even delving into the owners' archives (the Dundas/Zetland family archives held at North Yorkshire Archive Offices), no bill of sale or receipt exists for this piece.

With the benefit of twelve years more experience in identifying Chippendale's marquetry and the furniture he built, I acknowledge that the carcass is indeed an obvious example of Chippendale's Rococo style; almost identical to that built for Lady Winn's Bedchamber at Nostell Priory (c.1770) – see Figure 10.1. However, I am now able to identify the style of marquetry work, and in my opinion, it most certainly is not Chippendale's, but without a shadow of doubt, that of Pierre Langlois.

With that in mind, let me show the marquetry elements on this commode in comparison with other proven Langlois marquetry. Some of these elements are illustrated in Figures 4.2 to 4.5.

4 • THE LANGLOIS 'BRAND'

Figure 4.2* View of daisy-type flowers on the two matching doors, all set into fustic veneer background.

Figure 4.3* Close-up of flowers and green foliage.

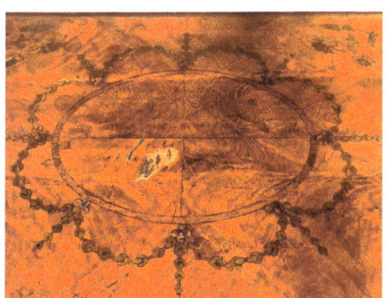

Figure 4.4* Top panel showing swags and drops of marquetry bellflowers – one of Langlois' popular motifs.

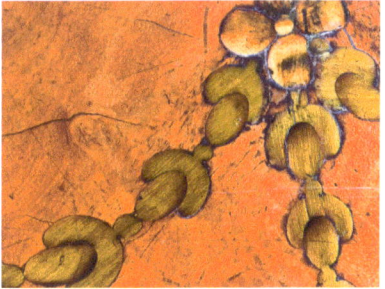

Figure 4.5* Close-up of bellflowers, showing how they got their name, resembling a church bell with the hammer hanging in the centre.

As you can see, integral to Langlois' designs are many floral arrangements, such as daisy-like flowers and bellflowers, which he used regularly across his marquetry designs. In essence they became part of his 'brand'.

LANGLOIS PIER TABLE AT TEMPLE NEWSAM HOUSE

To justify my assertion, it is worth looking closely at a piece of furniture securely attributed to Langlois. The pier table illustrated in Figures 4.6 and 4.7, made by Pierre Langlois and now on display at Temple Newsam House, Leeds, shows daisy-type flowers on the left and right of the table, typical of those seen on the Aske commode.

* Reproduced by kind permission of Aske Hall

Langlois repeated this style of marquetry throughout his career and, like Chippendale, he developed a distinctive number of motifs which became his trademark. These included, among others, combinations of daisy-type flowers, foliage, ribbons and bellflower swags and drops.

Figure 4.6* Commode made by Pierre Langlois on display at Temple Newsam House.

Figure 4.7* Here we see the close-up of the two matching drops of bellflowers hanging from the matching foliage left and right.

Figure 4.8* Close-ups of the clusters of flowers on each side of the table, designed as mirror images – another Langlois characteristic.

* By kind permission of Leeds Museums and Galleries

Langlois' marquetry techniques

Marquetry design prior to 1770 was constrained to some degree by the size of the motifs used. While that still leaves a wide choice of artistry (and clearly Langlois' designs were artistic and popular with his patrons, as his sales testify), we must remember the other practical constraint that was always present: namely, the size of the marqueteur's fretsaw.

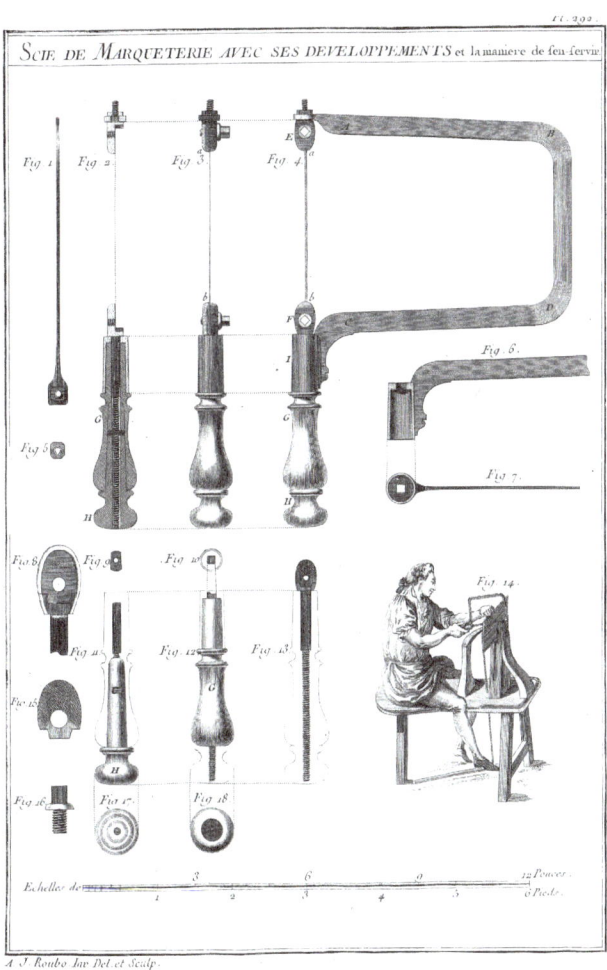

Figure 4.9 Engraved illustration from André Jacob Roubo's classic five-volume treatise 'L'Art du Menuisier' written between 1769 and 1775, showing a hand-held fretsaw used in Paris during the period. It also shows (bottom right) a man seated at a marquetry cutter's bench which allows him to hold the veneer in a foot-controlled clamp, while he cuts out the small-sized pattern with his hand-held fretsaw.

As an experienced specialist marqueteur, I can assure readers that for most of the 1760s the only fretsaw in use in London and, I suspect, in France, was of the kind illustrated in Figure 4.9. The length of the throat of the saw determines the size of motif that can be cut out, the throat being the distance between the frame of the saw and the saw blade. While the size of the saw's throat governs the size of motifs one can effectively cut, it does not explain how the background veneer was also cut to allow the sawn motifs to fit into it.

We have further evidence of this fretsaw in use in London: Figure 4.10 reproduces a late-18th-century painting showing two men performing marquetry work in a London workshop. In my first book *CCMR*, I said that the picture, by Swedish artist Elias Martin, was painted in 1760. That appears to be incorrect, as the Swedish National Museum, which owns the picture, now suggest it was painted between 1768 and 1771.

Further evidence of contemporary fretsawing techniques can be seen in this image; the man on the left is 'inlaying' the fretsawn marquetry elements into the veneer covering the circular table. How interesting it is to see that they consist of a border of small green foliate marquetry elements. We have to note here that the pieces could not be inlaid by fretsaw, since the

Figure 4.10
Two men performing marquetry work in London as painted by Swedish artist Elias Martin between 1768 and 1771

tiny saw seen in use by the man seated at the bench would not be anywhere near big enough to perform that process. Fretsawing large sheets of veneers required a treadle fretsaw. Note that the French equivalent of the treadle saw (the 'chevalet') did not appear until the early 1800s (probably around 1810).

In Martin's picture, the 'inlaying' (as marquetry work was called at this time) shows two men completing the two separate processes: one sawing and one inlaying.

We are lucky to have first-hand documentary evidence of the marqueteur's art in this painting by Elias Martin. Martin spent time in London with his uncle Georg Haupt (the renowned Swedish cabinet-maker) between 1768 and 1771. Prior to their arrival in London, they had first met in Paris along with fellow Swedish cabinet-maker Christopher Furlohg.

It appears that in the summer of 1766, Haupt's nephew (the painter Elias Martin), had arrived in Paris to join his two compatriots. Christopher Furlohg was the first of the three to move on to London. Elias Martin and Haupt followed either at the end of 1767 or early in 1768.[5]

The presence of Elias Martin in London in those particular years raise the tantalising question of which marqueteurs are the subject of his painting. This is a question I discuss later – in Chapter 9, see page 53. .

---

[5] *BIFMO: Haupt, Georg (1741–84) show published details*

CHAPTER FIVE

COLLABORATION AND PARTNERSHIP

Following the discovery of the origin of the Aske Commode marquetry, I was keen to examine as much of Pierre Langlois' past work as possible.

To start with I wanted to learn about brass foundry work and I came across an article in Christopher Gilbert's epic book *The Life and Works of Thomas Chippendale*. Here I found an intriguing yet unexpected link to Pierre Langlois:

> *Even some elaborate furniture mounts may have been acquired from trade sources since the corner brasses on a mahogany commode at Nostell (Fig. 227) precisely match those on furniture ascribed to Pierre Langlois, who appears to have commissioned them from Dominique Jean, his son-in-law.*[6]

Figure 5.1* Mahogany commode at Nostell Priory attributed to Thomas Chippendale (c.1770), showing brass mounts on the front legs.

---

[6] Gilbert, Christopher *The Life and Works of Thomas Chippendale*. Cassell Ltd, London, 1978, pp. 44–46

* Photo © National Trust / Robert Thrift

5 • COLLABORATION & PARTNERSHIP

Chippendale was already looking for a brass foundry owner in order to set up production of brass mounts to apply to his marquetry-decorated furniture. He found one in Dominique Jean who was about to open, or had already opened, a metal foundry in his father-in-law's workshop in Tottenham Court Road.

At this stage it was my belief that, around the mid 1760s, Chippendale made enquiries of Langlois' workshop regarding building a commode which included marquetry and decorative brass mounts.

This would be a joint working arrangement, where Chippendale would build the carcass, Langlois would be responsible for the design of the marquetry, and Jean would manufacture mounts from designs in wooden moulds provided by one of Chippendale's carvers.

I say this because I have it on good authority that some of Jean's own castings of brass furniture mounts made for his father-in-law were of sub-standard quality; this is an observation made by Thomas Lange and John Russell (both highly skilled furniture repairers and conservators working for Ronald Phillips Ltd, Mayfair, London). I imagine they have had more hands-on experience with Langlois' furniture than any other conservators over the years. It could be that Langlois used another foundry workshop before Jean married his daughter and set up his workshop in his father-in-law's establishment, or perhaps Jean was not a skilled carver and subsequently his metal mounts showed this. Perhaps Chippendale had also noted the sub-standard work himself and maybe suggested a solution, which would play to the strengths of both parties.

Langlois would also provide a suitable marquetry design for his marqueteurs to build. I believe that the Aske Commode is a prime example of this collaboration between Chippendale, Langlois and Jean. I estimate the completion of the build occurred around 1765/6, as Pierre Langlois died on 19th February 1767.

The commode now belongs to the Dundas family and is housed at Aske Hall, Yorkshire, England. So how did it end up there?

Following his death, the commode remained in Langlois' workshop. Langlois' widow, Tracey, organized two sales of works, the first in 1771 followed by a second sale a year later.

I believe that the Aske Hall Commode was one such piece.

These events are covered in a lengthy article written by historian Lucy Wood and published by the Furniture History Society, UK[7]. Wood records

---

[7] *Newsletter No 196, November 2014, pp 5&6 published by The Furniture History Society and written by Lucy Wood*

that the first sale was on 18–20 February 1771, at the premises of Mr Hogard & Co. in Savile Row. Included in the sale were:

> *A Great variety of fine pieces of cabinet-work, being some of the principal performances of that most ingenious workman Mr PETER LANGLOIS, cabinet-maker, in Tottenham-court-road, and are removed for the conveniency of sale; consisting of commodes, beaufets, writing and dressing tables, and various other articles of the most exquisite workmanship, beautifully inlaid with various sorts of wood, brass, tortoishell, &c. and richly embellished with grand chased ornaments in an elegant taste, and fit to furnish the most superb apartments. (The Gazetteer and New Daily Advertiser,* Friday 15 February 1771, quoted in Wood 2014, p.6)

Then, a year later on 24–25 February 1772, a two-day sale of further stock took place, at a near-identical address (possibly the same sale room):

> *Some most elegant and matchless Pieces of inlaid work, begun by that famous artist Mr. Peter Langlois, and finished since his decease. In this sale will be exhibited a pleasing variety of commodes, cabinets, dressing-tables &c. inlaid in the most elegant taste, and richly ornamented with or molu; particularly a cabinet, in the antique taste, finely vaneered with japan; a most beautiful lady's secretary, &c. several pieces of the or molu, in figures, candle branches, and various other ornaments, an elegant clock, inlaid with tortoiseshell, by Rimbault, models of ships, &c. &c. At the same time will be sold, some elegant houshold furniture, china, &c. likewise rich Burgundy and Madeira wines, samples of which then [sic] as above. (The Gazetteer and New Daily Advertiser,* Thursday 20 February 1772, quoted in Wood 2014, p.7)

It seems likely the Aske Commode could have been sold at one of these two sales and purchased by Sir Lawrence Dundas (or his agent), which would explain why no bill of sale exists. Neither have searches in archives or elsewhere provided any documentary evidence. We know that Sir Lawrence made earlier purchases of Langlois' furniture for his London, Edinburgh and Yorkshire homes, thus confirming the good relationship he had with the firm. Therefore, it is not unreasonable to assume the commode was purchased from one of these sales and subsequently held in Sir Lawrence's London home (19 Arlington Street), prior to its moving to Aske Hall, Yorkshire.

The commodes shown in Chapter 3 in Figures 3.12 and 3.14 may also have been disposed of at one these two sales. My reasoning for this stems from the Metropolitan Museum's published dates of delivery being given as 'circa 1771–73' and 'circa 1770-1780'. Clearly no bills of sale exist, and the dates given here are after Langlois' death in 1767.

CHAPTER SIX

KITTING OUT A MARQUETRY WORKSHOP

Astonishingly, Chippendale had produced no marquetry-decorated furniture we know of prior to Langlois' death in 1767.

During his visits to Langlois' workshops, Chippendale would have had ample visual evidence of what was needed to run a marquetry workshop, since Langlois had successfully produced marquetry since 1759. It would be helpful for me to explain here what Chippendale would have observed in Langlois' workshop.

Principally, space was needed for a number of separate processes: building the furniture, constructing the marquetry work and carrying out various finishing processes, and finally adding the engraving work to the finished marquetry that adds three-dimensional artistry to the design. This required several large tables to accommodate the various panels which made up each piece of furniture.

Within the marquetry construction area there would need to be room for performing fretsawing, inlaying, finishing and engraving.

Chippendale, as a talented furniture maker and ambitious designer, must have questioned how larger marquetry designs (which were to appear later in his marquetry furniture) would be handled if a larger fretsaw was not available. This was 1767 and it is my belief that the answer was to come in the following year or so.

DYEING VENEERS

In the 1770s, all London furniture makers in the St Martin's Lane area used dyed veneers extensively to embellish their marquetry work.

The process of dyeing veneers requires chemistry skills including; knowledge of mordants and modifiers (chemicals that assist dyeing by fixing colour into fibres), as well as how to effectively calculate and adjust the pH (power of Hydrogen) level of all the materials involved in the process. (In dyeing, the aim is to perform the process in a neutral or near-to-neutral scale (pH 7) as possible: for example, pure, demineralised water is essential for dyeing, achieved by being passing the water through a bed of ion-exchange resin which removes mineral salts.)

The physical process of dyeing veneers requires a vast amount of space to house huge vats (each holding multiple sheets of veneers), and a large drying area: collectively there would need to be space to dye and dry at least twelve different dye types (to cater for the range of colours needed to meet the demands of the London-based furniture industry at the time).

Because of the complexity of this process, I feel it safe to say that, rather than making and applying the dyes to the veneers themselves, Langlois and all other furniture makers in the district must have purchased their dyed veneer stocks from specialist suppliers.

In 2008, respected German conservator Heinrich Piening performed dye tests on eight different Chippendale commissions, using UV-VIS Spectronomy to analyse the substances used to create different dyes. From these tests, he was able to prove that five different yellow dyes were found, plus three different red dyes across the eight different Chippendale commissions.

Heinrich also tested a Pierre Langlois table held in Temple Newsam House, Leeds, for its dye contents. Not surprisingly the dyes found on Langlois' marquetry work were exactly the same types as used on the Chippendale pieces, indicating that the purchased dyed veneers were most likely from one single source. Full details of the research and tables of results can be found in Chapter 4 of *CCMR* (pp. 100–102).

CHAPTER SEVEN

DISCOVERING CHIPPENDALE'S MARQUETEURS

Following Gilbert's declaration about the source of the brass mounts on Chippendale and Langlois furniture, I started to search for more of Langlois' furniture which could have been completed around 1770. You can image my pleasant surprise when I found a pair of commodes both with the same matching brass mounts as the Nostell commode shown in Figure 5.1 on page 26.

THE 'PHILLIPS' COMMODES

This pair of Langlois matching commodes was being held in the furniture showrooms of Ronald Phillips Ltd, Mayfair, London. I could not believe my luck. I had visited the showrooms and workshops some years earlier when I was invited to assist Dr Heinrich Piening to perform dye tests on a Chippendale commode, a powerful piece of research outlined in *CCMR* (pp 259–63).

On 9th August 2021, I visited Ronald Phillips' showrooms for a second time to examine the commodes (shown in Figure 7.1) at first hand. I'm grateful to Simon Phillips (current owner), for giving me permission, and Thomas Lange (researcher, furniture restorer and conservator), who set up the meeting.

I made extensive examination of all the veneering and marquetry work to both pieces, and as a skilled Chippendale marquetry practitioner, I confirm the following opinion.

I have no doubt whatsoever that the marquetry work on these two commodes is the work of the same marqueteur who performed all the marquetry work on all of Chippendale's commissions which appear in my previous book *Chippendale's classic Marquetry Revealed*.

This immediately raises the question: how am I able to declare this statement simply by looking at it? My response is by application of my extensive knowledge and practice as a trained marqueteur, having spent

Figure 7.1 Matching pair of Commodes made by Pierre Langlois c.1770, examined while on sale by Roland Phillips, Mayfair showrooms, London.

7 • Discovering Chippendale's Marqueteurs

over twenty years examining the work of this man at close quarters and in stately homes and museums all across the UK). Having also built replica copies of two of Chippendale's prestigious marquetry pieces, I feel I have become familiar with, and learnt about, every aspect of the man's many skills.

In Figure 7.1, we see the front elevation of the two commodes, showing marquetry set into padauk veneer background, with kingwood crossbanding borders. The door panels are bordered with a single stringer and half-round berries, which, as we saw earlier, are shown in Chippendale's *Director* (see Figure 2.2 on page 4). The marquetry on the two doors of each piece forms a mirror image of each other, showing that the inlaid marquetry is inverted on one panel to create the artistic match.

The marquetry on the two side panels is also identical, but one side inverted to create a mirror image of its opposite side.

Just as you would expect, the same treatment is afforded to the two matching tops. The marquetry shown on Top 1 in Figure 7.2 is an almost exact mirror image of that shown on Top 2 in Figure 7.3. However, that's not where the similarity ends with the other panels, because the two rosewood background veneers (each joined down the centre of the tops) are also carefully selected to form mirror images of each other. The very stripy veneer on the bottom left-hand corner of Top 1, is matched by a similar-toned veneer on the bottom right-hand corner on Top 2, with the wood tone darkening towards the centre back of the commode tops.

Similarly, on the door fronts shown in Figure 7.1, you will notice one particularly dark background on each commode (on the right in the top one; on the left in the lower one). Again, they have been carefully selected and placed to enhance the mirror-image effect.

I have never before seen this mirroring technique applied so precisely to 18th-century marquetry work. There are certainly symmetrical panels within Chippendale's designs, which I have pointed out in *CCMR* and applauded as a key component of his approach; symmetry and balance are also features of marquetry by famous earlier furniture makers such as André-Charles Boulle (1642–1732) and Jean-François Oeben (1721–63). Langlois, however, goes one step further, by adding the mirror-image feature both to his marquetry work and (in the case of the two tops) to the background veneers as well.

The technique raises the question: was this near-exact matching achieved by the inlay method, or by the new two-part fretsawing method which was to arrive before the estimated delivery date (c. 1770) of these two commodes? The proof may never be truly found unless veneers are lifted to reveal the

Figures 7.2 (Top 1) and 7.3 (Top 2) show the mirrow-image marquetry of two commodes.

presence, or otherwise, of the use of the inlay knife, which leaves tell-tale knife marks on the substrates.

My own view is that it was achieved by inlaying, since that was the method used throughout Langlois' period of activity. These two commodes, and other incomplete commissions, still had to be finished following Langlois' death, as will be explained later.

My last and remaining question about this unique mirroring technique is: was this the inspiration of the designer, or of the inlayer experimenting with an innovative inlay trick? Since there are still other Langlois productions for me to see (at some time in the future) for the first time, I will leave the question unanswered.

Sight of heavy sandshading (as seen on the two central flowers, coloured blue and white) illustrates how impossible it was to keep the shading toned down when using sawn veneers as opposed to sliced veneers. Sawn veneers need longer exposure to the hot sand to achieve the colour change. In contrast, the delicate engraving to the foliage is totally sublime.

7 · Discovering Chippendale's Marqueteurs

However, above all that, the overall marquetry work shows great maturity and confidence in its application.

Listed in the Phillips catalogue associated with these matching commodes is the description given below.

A pair of George III ormolu mounted padauk, rosewood and kingwood marquetry commodes attributed to Pierre Langlois.

Note: The commodes retain the original brass mounts, apart from the central mount to the apron, which is a faithful restoration, using the original nail holes and copying the mount from another commode by Langlois.

English circa 1770

Dimensions:

Height 33 inch; 84 cm
Width: 43½ inch; 110.5 cm
Depth: 20¼ inch; 51.5 cm

Provenance:

William 6th Baron Craven (1738–1791)
By descent until 1965;
Robert Bradley Craven, 6th Earl of Craven (1917–1965) Sotheby's, 8 October 1965 lot 140;
Mallett & Sons Ltd, London, England;
Private collection, England;
Mallett and Sons Ltd, England;
Private collection, London, England.

Pierre Langlois used mounts produced by his son-in-law, Dominique Jean. The pattern of the central mount*, now reinstated, is consistent with those on other commodes by the same maker, between which there is scarcely any variation. The fact that the same fixing holes have been used further confirms that the mount chosen is correct.

A similar pair, only slightly differing in the door marquetry, was retained by Frank Partridge Inc. in 1935 as part of the Drury Collection in New York, USA. Another similar pair are to be found in a private collection in England and were shown at the Masterpiece Fair in London in 2011.

---

*The central mount to the apron, referred to above, was installed by John Russell, restorer and conservator to Ronald Phillips.

Figure 7.4 Commode showing three rosewood veneered drawers retaining the original ornate swan-neck handles

The inner veneering work (see Figure 7.4) is top-class. The matching padauk veneers laid in herringbone fashion on the two inner doors present a striking classic appearance, as do the rosewood veneers laid similarly on the three matching drawers. Padauk is used on all the crossbanding lines around and between the three drawers

Figures 7.5 to 7.7 show in more detail some of the marquetry techniques used by the expert craftsman.

Figure 7.5 Close-up of flowers on one of the commodes, with hints of green (indigo & yellow) dye still evident. Note the masterful engraving to the petals. Could this be performed by the marqueteur himself?

Figure 7.6 Interlocking ring and loop supporting roses and foliage on the side panels of the commodes. Note the heavy and dark sandshading, so typical when using sawn veneers in 18th-century marquetry.

7 · Discovering Chippendale's Marqueteurs

*Figure 7.7
Again dark/heavy shading, yet by contrast, the ultra-fine engraving applied to the green leaves below is typical of later work on Chippendale productions. The fretsaw cutting of the fringed petals at the top is masterfully executed.*

Figure 7.8 Brass casting (made by Dominique Jean) applied to both front legs, identical to those fitted to Chippendale's commode made for Nostell Priory (see Figure 5.1 on page 26).

Figure 7.9 Side profile of the brass casting

A SECOND PAIR OF MATCHING COMMODES

Illustrated in Figure 7.10 is one of another pair of matching commodes by Langlois, offered for sale on the website of Ronald Phillips Ltd (and since sold), who also supplied the photograph. There are subtle differences in the marquetry elements compared to the previous pair, shown in Figure 7.1. The ribbons on the two front doors are transposed to the bottom of the panels, and birds are introduced (one on each door). Each panel displays a different marquetry design, so no mirror imaging on this production. The quality of the marquetry work, however, is equal to that on the other pair, confirming in my view that the same marqueteur must have performed this work.

As with the previous pair of commodes, the brass castings (made by Dominique Jean) applied to both front legs are identical to those made for Nostell Priory (see Figure 5.1).

Having now examined in detail the marquetry on the four commissions described in Chapter 3, together with two pairs of commodes in this chapter, I am convinced that the technical skills shown across all these pieces bear the distinctive hallmarks of the work of one person. In short, I firmly believe: *'I have at last found my marqueteur'*

Figure 7.10 One of a pair of commodes by Langlois, showing the same quality of marquetry work as seen in Figure 7.1.

LANGLOIS' MARQUETRY STYLE

At this stage I need to explain why I am so certain this marquetry style belongs to Langlois and not to any of the other renowned furniture makers in the vicinity. It comes down to individuality and repetition of design. Initially, as we have seen, Langlois copied motifs found within Chippendale's *Director*, yet he used them in a style that none of his competitors used (including Chippendale himself).

Firstly looking at 'swags and drops', we can see an obvious difference. Compare the Langlois bellflowers reproduced in Figure 7.11 with the same motif as used by Chippendale (Figure 7.12). The contrast is strking. The same applies in the use of 'ribbons and loops'. Langlois' and Chippendale's styles are again very different (Figures 7.13 and 7.14).

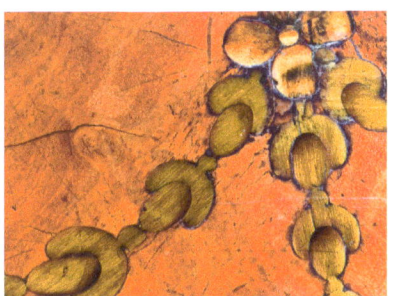

Figure 7.11 Langlois' swags and drops are barely changed from the motif design seen in the Director *(see Figures 2.6 and 2.7 on p. 6)*

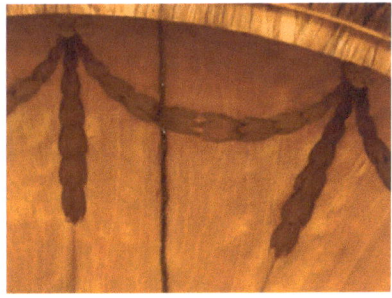

Figure 7.12 Chippendale's swags and drops seen here on the Diana & Minerva *commode, are converted into laurel leaf style foliage*

Figure 7.13 Langlois uses a ring and loop wrapped around the upper stringing, to hold up a cluster of flowers and foliage.

Figure 7.14 Door panel from Chippendale's Diana & Minerva *commode, uses a ribbon and loop to hold up the garland of foliage*

Figure 7.15*
Detail from Chippendale's 'Lunar' table, showing the archer's bow, quiver and torch, symbols of love and learning.

If you look back at Figure 3.13 on page 17, you will see that Langlois uses a ribbon and loop from which to 'hang' a torch, archers' bow and quiver with arrows (symbols of learning and love), together with foliage, stylistically a very impressive presentation. Langlois liked to tie his ribbon/loop artwork around the border stringing – a distinctive feature – one which Chippendale never used. However, he did use the same symbols (torch, bow and arrows) on the Lunar table in 1775 (see Figure 7.15). Oeben also used the same symbols as seen in Figure 3.5 on page 10.

These comparisons lead me to the impression that Langlois was thoroughly immersed in the *Director*, drawings from which he copiously copied. His realisations certainly did the drawings artistic justice and, clearly, his interpretations in marquetry proved highly popular with his wide customer base. Chippendale must also have been impressed when he visited Langlois' workshops and saw samples of his design work.

It is also important to remind ourselves that Langlois' marquetry career ended in 1767, two years before Chippendale started building his first marquetry creation (a games table for Nostell Priory, 1769).

The more I study Langlois' work, the more I admire his creative artistry, inspiring me to search out every piece he created during his very short productive eight-year career (1759–67). For him to die so young, at the age of 48, was a great loss to the industry.

Whilst the design of Langlois' motifs may have originated from Chippendale's *Director* drawings, he most certainly showed he could use them artistically within a marquetry context. Does this perhaps suggest that Langlois was teaching Chippendale how to express his creations? Langlois was clearly a very talented and productive cabinetmaker and designer, and, in my view, his work demands greater awareness, recognition and renown.

*Reproduced by kind permission of the private collector

CHAPTER EIGHT

NAMES: FINDING AN INLAYER AND AN ENGRAVER

Having made the mind-blowing discovery that Langlois' marqueteur was the same man who performed all Chippendale's marquetry work, I was hungry to name him.

It is perhaps important to record here that in the 18th century marqueteurs were called 'inlayers' (clearly because that is the technique they used to insert the marquetry elements into the substrates). The title 'marqueteur' arrived much later in the 20th century.

After extensive searches, five definitive records came to light.

The first is an article[8] from BIFMO (British and Irish Furniture Makers Online) which names an inlayer working for Langlois, as recorded in a signature on a marquetry panel on a commode made in 1770.

Dutton, H. (or M.) (1770)

Dutton, H. (or M.), address unrecorded, inlayer (c. 1770). Signed a marquetry panel on a commode attributed to P. Langlois. [Burlington, June 1980, p. 416]

The original entry from Dictionary of English Furniture Makers, 1660-1840 can be found at British History Online.

The second is a further article from BIFMO[9]:

Dutton, M. (century)

Location unknown; furniture maker (fl. second quarter of the 18th century)

There are four brass-inlaid commode chests of drawers, made during the second quarter of the eighteenth-century at Buckingham Palace, three of which bear 'signatures' including that of M. Dutton.

Source: Boynton, 'The Moravian Brotherhood and the Migration of Furniture Makers in the Eighteenth Century', Furniture History (1993)

---

[8] *https://bifmo.history.ac.uk/entry/dutton-h-or-m-1770*

[9] *https://bifmo.history.ac.uk/entry/dutton-m-century*

The third finding is different – this time not of an inlayer, but of an engraver – and is from the Royal Collection Trust at www.rtc.uk[10]. Here is recorded the following about a piece in the collection:

Commode c 1763, one of a pair, which forms a set of four in the Royal Collection. All four commodes are inscribed on the tops and of those one is signed J M Dutton who is listed as an 'Engraver'. The commode does not include marquetry, but they are veneered on the front with rosewood. Another engraver also signed his name F M LA Cave (in reverse). François Morellon La Cave is recorded as an etcher and engraver and is presumed to have joined Langlois for this apparently unprecedented commission. Among the émigrés working for Langlois was his son-in-law, the bronze founder and mount-maker Dominique Jean, who may have made the exceptional mounts on these commodes.

If this is the same Mr Dutton, he clearly appears to have dual skills; he has signed one commode in 1770 which includes marquetry work for which he was named as an inlayer, and another in 1763 (which has no marquetry work), where he has been named as an engraver.

How interesting to see him recorded as an engraver; this would make sense for this commode, because marquetry does not appear on the piece whereas engraving on brasswork does, on the commode top. It would have been useful if Mr Dutton had these dual skills, as the two signatures suggest.

Fourthly, a further record appeared naming a second man. On a visit to Ronald Phillips Ltd, Thomas Lange (researcher and furniture conservator), pointed me to an entry in Christopher Gilbert's book[11], where another Langlois commode is signed by a 'Mr Zurn' (see Figure 8.1):

'Pictorial Dictionary of Marked London Furniture', page 502 – image 1034, which states:

'Zurn: commode, one of a pair, marquetry on a kingwood ground, c1765, attributed to Pierre Langlois, Zurn is believed to have been a specialist inlayer in the Langlois workshop, signed. National Trust, The Vyne, Hampshire.'

The commode itself is illustrated in Figures 8.1 and 8.2. Figure 8.2 shows the flowing floral design characteristic of Langlois' marquetry. Once again, the drawer fronts display mirror-image symmetry, with the design to the left of each central escutcheon being an exact reflection of the design to the right of it.

---

[10] *https://bifmo.history.ac.uk/entry/dutton-j-m-1763*

[11] Gilbert, Christopher *Pictorial Dictionary of Marked London Furniture, 1700–1840, 1996*

8 · NAMES: FINDING AN INLAYER & AN ENGRAVER

Figure 8.1* One of a pair of commodes at The Vyne, Hampshire, attributed to Langlois. According to the National Trust's information sheet: 'It is likely that they were supplied for John Chute's London house and brought to The Vyne by his heir, Thomas Lobb Chute.'

Figure 8.2* Close-up of the marquetry on the commode front, typical of Langlois' style.

* *Photo ©National Trust Images / James Mortimer*

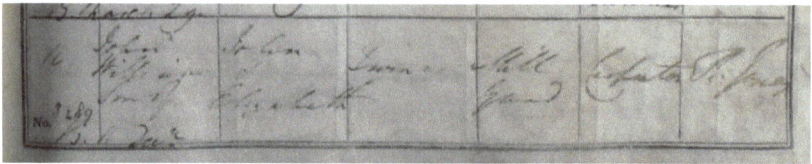

Figure 8.3 1810 baptismal record of John William Zurn, St Giles' Cripplegate, London

I have not been able to track down further archival material relating to this Zurn, but a record does exist of the baptism of a John William Zurn (the son of John and Elizabeth Zurn), in St Giles' Cripplegate, London, in 1810. (The copy of the record is shown in Figure 8.3.)

Here, the father's profession is given as 'Carpenter'.

Now that is interesting! I'm surmising that the infant's father could be the son of Langlois' 'Mr Zurn'. Since John is the Christian name of both father and infant, it would be reasonable to suppose that the grandfather – possibly our inlayer Zurn – was also called John (or possibly Johann, if he was a German immigrant). While this evidence is inferential, it does clearly show that there was a woodworking Zurn family active in Georgian London.

Tantalisingly, these pieces of evidence give us the names of two men working as inlayer and engraver, both associated with the Langlois workshop. Could one of these men (or both working together), be the craftsmen who executed the superb fretwork, inlaying and engraving on Chippendale's marquetry furniture? I have already identified that the same marqueteurs who built the Langlois marquetry also built Chippendale's marquetry work.

My own belief is that they are Chippendale's marquetry team!

It is a shame Chippendale never signed any of his own work, nor were any other names ever found on any of his furniture.

ONE INLAYER OR TWO?

Marquetry constructed by the 'inlay' method allows for two men to fulfil the work: one to fret saw the motifs, while the other inlays them into the background veneer, as seen in the contemporary painting of the 'Ebenistes' (see Figure 4.10). This means that the work is performed quickly (which benefits output), but the labour costs are obviously doubled. The technique also limited the type and size of designs used; only small motifs which fitted the size of a hand-held fretsaw could be used, and up to about 1770, this was the case throughout Europe.

The alternative method is when marquetry is doubly sawn, using the 'two-part fretsawing' method. This technique can be completed by one man, but the time is doubled, which means construction is slower, and so again the cost is doubled.

Both techniques result in achieving tight joints between mating edges, which is always the desired result.

However, Chippendale wanted to introduce large designs with large motifs (such as long acanthus leaves, vases and urns, etc.), so he needed a much larger fretsaw. One such saw was to arrive just in time: the treadle fretsaw. This changed the marquetry industry throughout London, and Chippendale (as we are about to discover) had the finest and most skilful marqueteurs to perform the work for him.

Arrival of the treadle fretsaw

Figure 8.4 shows a replica floor-standing treadle fretsaw as used by London furniture makers in the mid to late 18th century. The whole saw, as used at the time, probably measured 183 cm (6 ft) high, by 102 cm (3 ft 4 in) wide. The sawyer would stand on one foot, using the other to operate the treadle. The size of the saw table allowed the inlayer to saw much larger motifs and background veneers than had previously been possible.

*Figure 8.4
A replica floor-standing treadle fretsaw. I also provide a technical drawing of the saw on pp. 38–9 of CCMR*

Redeploying inlayers and engraver

My initial thinking in my previous book (*CCMR*), that Chippendale's marquetry was performed by a marqueteur working for an external workshop, provides a new dilemma with the discovery of Messrs Dutton and Zurn. This I find extremely intriguing, since I have now found the men working for Langlois – or, to be precise, in his workshop.

Was it possible that Chippendale made a unique business arrangement with Langlois' widow and her son, Daniel Langlois, who took over the running of the workshop following his father's death, not as the trained cabinet maker he already was, but as an apprentice brass-caster working for his brother-in-law, Dominique Jean? This arrangement would have allowed the inlayers and engraver to remain working in Langlois' workshop and carry out all Chippendale's marquetry work without moving premises.

So many benefits could be gained by such an arrangement. Firstly, Chippendale would not have had to provide workshop space for carrying out marquetry construction. Secondly, Langlois' workshop in Tottenham Court Road was within easy walking distance (only one mile away) from Chippendale's workshop in St Martin's Lane. Thirdly, Chippendale's brass mounts would also be manufactured under the same roof.

There is another explanation which is more to do with the business situation Langlois' widow (Tracey Langlois) found herself in, following her husband's death in 1767. All new commissions would have ceased, yet there would have been a backlog of orders still to be finished. I have highlighted quite a number in this book; all the commodes with a delivery date of c1770 were clearly not completed by 1767, including the two sets of matching commodes shown in Chapter 7 (Figures 7.1 and 7.10), and the two commodes at the Metropolitan Museum featured in Chapter 3 (see Figures 3.12 and 3.14).

What I am illustrating here is that the Langlois family would have had the upper hand in deciding the fate of their marquetry staff's future, both from a practical point of view and the more pressing financial business need. With a very experienced and talented marquetry team, alongside the proven bronze/brass worker in Dominique Jean (who has now added Langlois' son Daniel to his team), this workforce now provided a very attractive business to its prestigious customers.

In short, Chippendale would have been presented with a *fait accompli*, but one which suited perfectly his immediate and long-term needs.

One question this arrangement does answer is, why historians and myself have never found the names of the inlayers and engraver working for Chippendale. The answer is that he never employed these men. Instead, he paid for their services, commission by commission. As it turned out it was the most practicable answer of all.

However, the question arises as to the longevity of such an arrangement. I again refer to the paper written by Lucy Wood[12], who examined the St Pancras paving rate books (which start in 1773) and discovered that Tracey Langlois continued to pay the rates on the Tottenham Court Road premises until 1773. The payments were then taken over by her son Daniel Langlois from 1774 to 1781, followed by her son-in-law Dominique Jean for the period 1782 to 1786. By 1787 the house was empty. Tracey Langlois herself died in 1781.

That period more than covers the career of Chippendale the Elder which ended in 1775. Thomas Chippendale the Younger, however, continued the business until 1796. So clearly Messrs [John] Zurn, J M Dutton, Daniel Langlois and Dominique Jean (if still working in 1786), would have had to move premises, or take on the rental themselves.

---

[12] *Wood, Lucy (2014) 'New light on Pierre Langlois (1718–1767)', The Furniture History Society Newsletter No. 196, November 2014, pp.1–7*

CHAPTER NINE

RESOLVING THREE CHIPPENDALE MARQUETRY SITUATIONS

I estimate that the Langlois/Chippendale working arrangement (as just detailed) would have commenced in late 1767, or at the very latest mid-1768. I reason this because Chippendale commenced designing and building marquetry-decorated furniture around this time. As previously stated, his first commission was the Games Table delivered to Nostell Priory in 1769.

With delivery of the treadle fretsaw, and discovery of the named marquetry team, I can now address matters I raised in CCMR, regarding three marquetry 'situations' which Chippendale and his marqueteurs encountered.

1 THE HAREWOOD LIBRARY WRITING TABLE

I refer to the table built for Harewood House c.1770 and now owned by the Leeds Museums and Galleries. In 2004, I built a replica of one of the door panels as part of a project linked to the restoration of the original table. A detailed description of that project is given in Chapter 5 of my previous book, *CCMR*.

There, I explained that the marquetry on the door panels of the four matching doors had been built using the 'packet fretsawing' method. This is where the veneers for the leaf motifs were cut at the same time as the background veneer.

This technique required one holly veneer dyed green, and one Indian rosewood background veneer. Both veneers were held together with tiny pins, with the design pasted on the top veneer. This formed the 'packet' to be fretsawn. Figures 9.1 to 9.4, taken from *CCMR* illustrate the process.

Figure 9.4 shows the background veneer which should have been pre-cut to match the exact size of the door panel it was to be glued to. Clearly,

9 • RESOLVING THREE CHIPPENDALE MARQUETRY SITUATIONS

Figure 9.1 The design is repeated left to right, which means it can be separated down the middle prior to fretsawing. The two halves of the packet before inverting to form one packet.

Figure 9.2 The contents of the 'packet' for the acanthus leaves: two green-dyed veneers with the design pasted on, plus two Indian rosewood veneers.

Figure 9.3 Here we see the 'packet' being fretsawn. This picture was taken in 2004, when I owned a French-style saw (called a Chevalet). I have since replaced it with a treadle saw.

Figure 9.4 The finished product showing the matching green foliage let into the background veneer.

49

Figure 9.5*
Unfortunately, when Chippendale's marqueteurs offered the finished marquetry panel to the door panel, it proved to be too big. As seen here the tip of the acanthus leaf (circled) measuring 10 mm (3/8 in) had to be cut off.

* Reproduced by kind permission of Leeds Museums and Galleries

this step was omitted, and once the panel had been fretsawn and assembled, it became too late to undo! This became a 'defining moment' in the marquetry production.

To have to cut short two parts of the designer's work (both the left and right sides of the panels) was clearly a step too far. As a result of this, packet fretsawing was never practised again by Chippendale.

Instead, the technique was replaced by the more advanced practice of two-part fretsawing. I did remark at the time I published *CCMR* (in 2018), that the mistake was most likely attributed to the fact that the marqueteurs worked remotely from the cabinetmakers (*CCMR* p.129). How right I was, yet never for a minute did I envisage the situation I have uncovered in researching this publication only three years later.

2 THE TREADLE FRETSAW'S SHORTCOMING

The second 'mistake' I discovered whilst building a replica copy of the prestigious Diana & Minerva Commode (which had been made for Harewood House in 1773) concerned the newly acquired treadle fretsaw. The marqueteurs could not fretsaw the acanthus leaves (shown on the four matching quadrants in Figure 9.6), because the saw's throat was not big enough to accommodate the large distances each quadrant presented (which amounted to a diagonal measurement of over 2 ft (64 cm).

9 • Resolving Three Chippendale Marquetry Situations

Figure 9.6: The panel (shown here in a replica made by the author), measures 2200 mm (7 ft 4 in) wide and 600 mm (2 ft) deep, the largest panel ever designed by Chippendale.

It is appropriate at this point to explain the dilemma faced by myself, Chippendale and his marqueteur when realising that the treadle fretsaw throat was not large enough to saw the background veneers to allow the long-flowing acanthus leaves to be inserted (as I explain in *CCMR* Chapter 6, pp. 173–4). I estimated that the throat of his saw was 46 cm (1 ft 6 in), which has proved to be true. I also assumed that all marquetry work was performed by an independent marquetry workshop, which therefore forced Chippendale to resolve the problem himself. He did this by designing the

Figure 9.7: Distance ignoring the diamond

Figure 9.8: Distance with diamond added

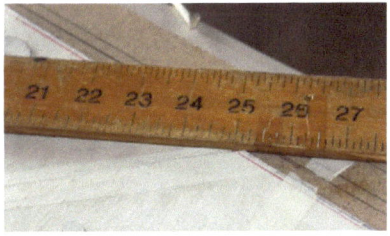

Figure 9.9: Distance over 2 ft

Figure 9.10: Distance reduced to 1 ft 6 inch

most impressive diamond shaped banding which allowed him to reduce the distance from over 2 ft to 1 ft 6 in on each of the four quadrants, which in turn allowed the throat of the fretsaw to complete the work.

The four images shown in Figures 9.7 to 9.10 display the measurements, first ignoring the diamond (Figures 9.7 and 9.9), followed by the result with the diamond added (Figures 9.8 and 9.10).

I suspect Chippendale would not have enjoyed making this enforced change. The whole design of the marquetry on this magnificent masterpiece demonstrates style, movement and curvature. There is not a straight geometric shape to be found anywhere. Speaking as a practitioner, I totally sympathise with him, but isn't it always the unforeseen that spoils the dream design?

Now that I know that the saw belongs to the two marqueteurs based in Tottenham Court Road, it is personally gratifying to discover that my initial thinking about ownership of the fretsaw was perfectly correct.

3 ARTWORK APPLIED TO THE COMMODE DRAWER FRONTS

Whilst investigating the original marquetry on the Diana and Minerva Commode in Harewood House (as I explain in *CCMR* pp. 83 & 84), I discovered the use of two different styles of engraving: not only the traditional method using an engraver's tool, but a second method using Indian ink applied with an artist's brush. An example of this type of engraving is shown in Figure 9.11, part of the central drawer-front of the Diana and Minerva Commode. We can identify it as the brush-and-ink method because some of the engraving has worn away through constant rubbing.

This discovery led me to the conclusion that Chippendale must have employed a second marquetry inlayer over and above those who worked on

Figure 9.11*
Here we see part of the swag of laurel leaves as they are today on the centre drawer of the Diana & Minerva Commode, showing erosion of the engraving artwork.

* Reproduced by the kind permission of the 7th Earl of Harewood Will Trust and the Trustees of the Harewood House Trust

9 • RESOLVING THREE CHIPPENDALE MARQUETRY SITUATIONS

the commode's main panels. Having now found Messers Zurn and Dutton (who performed the marquetry and engraving work) the question arises; did Chippendale employ yet another team to build the decoration to drawer fronts, and if so, who and why?

My response is 'yes'; another team was used to build drawer fronts. Otherwise, they would have been engraved in the same way; using an engraver's tool to match the engraving work on the rest of the marquetry panels. This situation only arises when drawers are included in the design, because they are a transportable part of the furniture and can therefore be farmed-out to speed up production.

From my research for CCMR, I found that eight commissions had marquetry-decorated drawers. This amounts to almost one third of Chippendale's total output. As for why a second team was needed and who it was; in order to help reduce the workload on the main marquetry team, perhaps Messers Zurn and Dutton advised on known colleagues.

My mind switches to Elias Martin's painting of the ébénistes (shown in Figure 4.10), which shows two men performing fretsawing and inlay work. The man seated at the saw bench appears to be very young (suggesting an apprentice), whilst the man inlaying appears to be middle aged.

I have evidence on the historic movement of the painting. According to Daniel Prytz, Curator at the Swedish National Museum in Stockholm, records show that Elias Martin kept the painting in his possession until the early part of the 19th century. It stayed in the hands of private collectors until the Swedish National Museum bought the painting in 1890 for 91 kronor. Following Daniel Prytz's check on the documentation held with the museum, no mention of the names of those portrayed is shown.

I had hoped that the men portrayed might be those working in Pierre Langlois' workshop, because Langlois was known to have working associations with many Swedish furniture makers and designers. These included Martin's uncle, Swedish furniture-maker Georg Haupt, as well as Christopher Furlohg and architect Sir William Chambers. Langlois clearly enjoyed the Swedish link as he occasionally used the Swedish spelling of his name, 'Petter'. Maybe Elias Martin was prompted by his uncle to visit Langlois' widow, on their return from Paris in late 1767 or 1768, and offer his condolence, which resulted in his performing a painting of his marqueteurs?

Sadly, no firm evidence has come to light about the names of those portrayed, but perhaps the above is a plausible suggestion. Despite that, the fact that it was painted in London during Martin's residence 1768–1780, serves as pictorial evidence of the tools used and techniques being practised to perform marquetry work in London in the important period of my research.

CHAPTER TEN

Lady Winn's Commode – Nostell Priory c.1770

My final contribution to this staggering discovery has to be the marquetry commode which Thomas Chippendale designed for Lady Winn's bedchamber at Nostell Priory. The reason for including it here is that I am confident the *carcass* was built either at the same time as, or very soon after, the production of the Aske Commode described in Chapter 4. I imagine this may have been the thinking of the furniture historian Lucy Wood in her comprehensive book *Catalogue of Commodes*[13], and also curators Adam Bowett and James Lomax, that led them to include the piece in the Chippendale Tercentenary Exhibition held at Leeds Museum in 2018. Placing the two commodes next to each other (as seen in Figures 10.1 and 10.2) illustrates the clear similarities between the two.

Figure 10.1*
Lady Winn's commode at Nostell Priory, marquetry by Chippendale

*By kind permission of Nostell Priory © National Trust

Figure 10.2†
The Aske Commode at Aske Hall, marquetry by Langlois

† By kind permission of Aske Hall

---

[13] *Lucy Wood Catalogue of Commodes*, London: HMSO Publications, 1994

Both designs follow the rococo theme with the sweeping bombe shapes across the fronts, so typical of French architecture of the early to mid-18th century. Also note the prominent brass mounts on both, which bear the hallmarks of Dominique Jean's early castings. However, that's where the similarity ends, or does it? Yes, the Chippendale marquetry design is easily recognisable (in Figure 10.1), as is that of Langlois (in Figure 10.2), but both designs emanate from the same source; Chippendale's *Director*. However, Langlois finished making furniture three years before Chippendale delivered his first marquetry commission, so who influenced whom is the question, which is perhaps the best way to leave this enchanting conundrum?

Looking at the stylistic differences between the decoration on the two pieces, however, does question why the marquetry on the Aske piece was not judged to be made by Langlois. As I have also shown, the Metropolitan Museum did not identify the distinctive work of Langlois on the two commodes shown in Chapter 3 in Figures 3.12, 3.13 and 3.14 (pages 16–18).

I have highlighted the similarity of design between Chippendale's marquetry and that of Langlois and the link to the *Director* which bonds their marquetry designs. In turn, this prompted me to examine the facts more closely, leading to my discovery of the obvious links between the *Director* motifs, marquetry work, ormolu mounts and the personnel involved in their respective construction.

I believe that, without the hands-on training I have had, I could not have made these discoveries. As any furniture conservator will tell you, most of the clues as to a maker are to be found in the materials and construction techniques within the piece. Similarly, those same principles apply to the design and application of marquetry work.

Sadly, hands-on furniture making skills are only taught today in privately run colleges. The teaching of furniture-making in national council funded colleges (as found in cities and most large towns across the western world), had ceased by about 2010. In the UK, this was mainly due to the change in funding by the City & Guilds Institute who set the educational funding levels to furniture-making colleges across the UK. All this came about because of a change in manufacturing techniques which witnessed the introduction of computer-driven machinery, known as CNC (Computer Numerical Control), which obviated the necessity to teach traditional hand and machine skills. Computer-driven marquetry cutting (using a laser), arrived soon after, which changed the industry worldwide. This means the passing down of traditional skills (as I have been privileged to receive, teach and write about) looks to be sadly gone and lost in the future.

CNC-constructed furniture is today's 'brand' and across Europe, the biggest playmaker of this brand being Ikea, who produce high-quality, flat-packed, self-assembly furniture for homes and offices. I have to admit that I have succumbed to purchasing several pieces for my own home – a handsome bookcase, a work desk, and an extendable dining table, all made of oak. Furthermore, Ikea also back up their products with an illustrated catalogue showing all the ranges of furniture, just as Chippendale's flagship *Director* did nearly 250 years ago. The only difference is that Ikea's catalogue is online and reaches a vastly wider audience.

While I salute the Ikea brand and its success, I do question whether it will last another 250 years and whether individual items – like pieces of Chippendale and Langlois furniture – will attract six- and seven-figure sums in furniture showrooms and auction houses across the world!

CHAPTER ELEVEN

My Marquetry Education

To end this book, I feel it worth giving some details about my marquetry education and the high level of hands-on education I gained, which totally changed my skill factor in the world of Chippendale marquetry.

After I took early retirement at age fifty, my late uncle-in-law, Tommy Limmer (forever known to me as 'Uncle Tommy') – a retired engineer whose skills also included cabinetmaking, woodturning, woodcarving, finishing, and marquetry – suggested I could do with a hobby in retirement! His proposal was to teach me marquetry (a term I had never heard before). This marquetry training offered by a man who was a woodworking and well-read genius lasted a full eight years.

During those intensive years, my craving hands learned so many in-depth marquetry skills under the benign tutorship of Uncle Tommy. We visited Harewood House (a treasure trove of everything to do with Chippendale) many times during this time, along with many other great houses containing Chippendale's furniture.

Tommy taught me how Chippendale's individual designs were constructed, and this is when my specialist training started.

I learned about each individual marquetry technique, and Tommy explained how they would have been adopted by the journeymen who performed the work. As an example, he showed me how Chippendale's iconic 'fans' would have been constructed, and how the multiple copies needed in Chippendale's production line were easily made, such that each fan was the exact same size and shape, by using a template. This 'Template Method' became a future teaching tool which I used over many years training students at Leeds College of Art and Design, and at York College.

Other key techniques included (of course) fretsawing and sandshading. Learning Chippendale's innovative two-part fretsawing method later became key to me being able to identify and 'read' his work at close quarters.

Uncle Tommy passed away in 1998, aged 83. It was through his patient mentoring and the passing on of his lifelong skills as a craftsman that I proudly became the proficient marqueteur I am recognised as today. Sadly, he never lived to see examples of my replica Chippendale marquetry (see below) nor the books he inspired.[14]

REPLICA PIER TABLE – BOOK TUTORIAL

Built by John Apps, then Head of Furniture Department at York College, with marquetry added by the author, this table was included in our book titled *The Marquetry Course*, published by Batsford in 2003 and now republished in 2020 under the new title *The Classic Marquetry Course*.

The first edition was successfully launched in 2004 at Harewood House, at the invitation of Lord Harewood, who allowed his beautiful Chippendale-furnished home to be the venue for the event. Following this, the table spent five years in the house for the visiting public to see and enjoy, and watch a video I made showing the construction of the marquetry work.

Figure 11.1 Replica Chippendale pier table. Instructions on how to build and decorate this table are given in 'The Classic Marquetry Course' (Mectcalfe & Apps 2020).

---

[14] Jack Metcalfe *Chippendale's Classic Marquetry Revealed*, 2018;
Jack Metcalfe & John Apps *The Classic Marquetry Course*, 2020

11 • My Marquetry Education

The Replica Diana & Minerva Commode

Chippendale's iconic masterpiece made in 1773 for Harewood House, attracted a colleague of mine (who wishes to remain anonymous) to build a replica copy, having seen the original when he attended our book launch at Harewood House in 2004. His masterful replica stands as testament to his supreme cabinetmaking skills which are clearly visible. I was then able to add the challenging marquetry work which I have detailed in depth in *CCMR*, Chapter 6. These can be seen in Figures 11.2, 11.3 and 11.4.

*Figure 11.2
The replica Diana
& Minerva Commode,
with marquetry constructed by
the author and veneered throughout
with synthetically dyed colours, which will
remain colourfast for life.*

Of all the work I have performed in my marquetry career, this stands out as my finest and most satisfying achievement. Now that I know the names and the background of the men who performed the iconic work to the original, makes it even more satisfying and personal. German specialist inlayer, [John] Zurn, alongside British engraver (and perhaps also inlayer) J.M. Dutton, who demonstrated their immense skills and artistry in their respective trades. I cannot begin to describe the joy it gives me to first identify them in person, then by their names, their nationalities and finally their workshop location. It just cannot get better than that!

Figure 11.3 Diana on the right door and Minerva left door, with the classic domed door in the centre. A dominance of pink fans and green foliage set into gold coloured satinwood.

Figure 11.4 Top panel showing the elaborate two-toned circular fan, which proved a sheer joy to build. The green dyed foliage is repeated in each of the four quadrants, which allowed me to fretsaw four veneers at one cutting, yet still having to saw each background veneer separately to produce the windows to accept the sawn elements.

REPLICA PIER TABLE TOP

Figure 11.5 shows my replica of the top of the pier table made originally for the Circular Dressing Room at Harewood House. The image shows the full extent of the proven colours following Heinrich Piening's UV-VIS Spectronomy tests of the original marquetry work, as detailed in *CCMR*, Chapter 7.

On completion of all the marquetry inlaying, which took me a full year, the table was polished by Philippa Barstow – furniture polisher and teacher in her Manchester studios. I then commissioned the leading Yorkshire

Figure 11.5 Shows a central panel, flanked by matching end panels, each covered in harwood-treated sycamore veneers and classic style marquetry work, illustrating how the original would have looked when first delivered to Harewood House in 1772.

engraver, Malcolm Long, to apply the all-important three-dimensional engraving work to the whole of the assembled marquetry. I am proud to announce that Malcolm Long's engraving perfectly echoes the extensive engraving work applied to the original.

This dynamic contribution of Thomas Chippendale's original table, plus my replica top, were both eagerly welcomed by Lucinda Compton (artistic conservator of furniture and fittings) for display in her family's

Figure 11.6 The two matching end panels, only electronically separated from the central panel, illustrates the sublime feminine colour scheme.

ancestral home, Newby Hall, for the Chippendale Tercentenary Exhibition in 2018. The table was displayed alongside the replica Diana & Minerva Commode (see above) for the whole of the summer months, and I was delighted to give three weekly talks to members of the public in Newby Hall's famous Tapestry Room, which was furnished by Chippendale himself. This was truly a great honour.

In Figure 11.6, we clearly see the feminine colour of pink applied to the decorative fans on the two matching end panels.

It is ironic that this was the only commission made by Chippendale which involves the one technique used constantly by Langlois' marquetry team under his leadership – namely inlaying. Also, it was the only commission for which Chippendale elected to use harwood[15]-stained sycamore veneers, which I prelaid to the substrate, using the original 18th century hammer-veneering[16] technique.

My Discovery of the Lunar Table

I made a ground-breaking discovery about this table, which prompted me to write a paper which was published by the Furniture History Society (FHS) on the 17th November 2009. This is my paper published again for your viewing.

CHIPPENDALE TRIBUTE TO THE LUNAR SOCIETY

Pursuing a passion is ample reason for any researcher to justify spending fifteen years committed to one subject. Such is the case with my pursuit of Thomas Chippendale's marquetry techniques. The knowledge gained has been invaluable, but now, added to that knowledge lies an unexpected surprise. I believe a hitherto unknown fact has emerged surrounding a

---

[15] *'Harwood', formally known as 'Harewood', describes the method of staining veneers different shades of grey. I discovered the correct name in 2016, while on a visit to Leeds Museum, where a list of 'Origins of place names in and around Leeds' showed the origin of Harewood as 'the grey wood'. Further searches revealed it derived from the Anglo-Saxon word 'har' means 'grey wood' where wood was initially spelt 'wudu', which eventually changed to wood. The word 'harwood' represents a gathering of trees as found in a wood or forest, where the presence of iron-rich soil changes the colour of the tree's bark to grey. CCMR p. 26 refers. Further research revealed that iron-rich soil exists generally between the county of Derbyshire and the southern Scottish borders.*

[16] *The technique of hammer-veneering is visually demonstrated at the start of my nine-minute YouTube video, showing how I constructed the marquetry on the replica curved-back pier table made initially for the Circular Dressing Room at Harewood House. https://youtu.be/pGd-kiL9_pBM*

11 • My Marquetry Education

Figure 11.7* The Lunar Table made for Harewood House 1775, now in a private collection. The original vibrant colours of the marquetry have been recreated electronically.

marquetry pier table made for Harewood House in 1775. The table (now in a private collection) was originally supplied along with matching oval girandoles and mirror glasses (also in private collections) for the Yellow Drawing Room.

Earlier this year I read an utterly fascinating book, *The Lunar Men: the friends who made the future* by Jenny Uglow (Faber & Faber, 2002). It posed questions to me regarding elements of the furniture and fittings destined for the Yellow Drawing Room. Perhaps a more compelling and cohesive programme was purposefully planned at the design stage, hinting that an untold story lurks within the room's original purpose.

'The Lunar Men' were a group of eighteenth-century philosophers and businessmen based in and around Birmingham, who met monthly at each other's houses on the Sunday nearest the full moon, such that the path home would be lit for them following their lengthy deliberations. These men and their unique discoveries and inventions undeniably formed the foundations for the 'Industrial Revolution'. Their names sound like a list of 'who's who' for the period: James Watt — pioneer of the steam engine; Josiah Wedgwood — leading potter; Joseph Priestley — preacher/philosopher who discovered oxygen and nitrogen as by-products of fire and air; Erasmus Darwin (grandfather of Charles) doctor, poet and philosopher whose book *The Botanic Garden* preceded his grandson's theory on evolution; Scotsman James Keir, chemist, inventor and industrialist; Thomas Day,

*Reproduced by kind permission of the private collector

Figure 11.8* The marquetry top as it looks today, the vibrancy of the original colours having been lost through fading.

poet whose dedicated efforts to end Britain's slave trade preceded that of William Wilberforce; and finally Matthew Boulton, industrialist, whose manufactory at Soho, Birmingham produced James Watt's steam engine.

These philosophers and industrialists, who worked together between c.1765 and 1803, had far-reaching connections with the Lascelles family, owners of Harewood House.

The pier table, set into a background of East Indian satinwood (*Chloroxylon swietenia*), crossbanded with South American tulipwood (*Dalbergia variabilis*), displays four radial panels set into purpleheart (*Fabaceae peltogyne*) backgrounds that run across the table, each separated by five ivory heads. A sixth ivory head is set into a lunette fan at the rear of the design. The lunette-shaped table stands on six stylishly carved legs and fluted plinth with small paterae. The plinth and legs, like the matching girandoles and mirror glasses were silver gilded, a material not previously used by Chippendale, nor used since.

The lunette shapes and choice of gilding material are significant because I believe that collectively they made a deliberate statement: forming a tribute to the Lunar Society, the gilding meant to invoke the silvery moon. Yellow damask on the Drawing Room walls was again a deliberate choice since it made the perfect foil for the silvered furnishings.

The four radial panels each have emblems which have symbolic meaning. Working from left to right in Figure 11.7, the first shows the tambour, triangle and pipe, depicting the muse presiding over dance. In the second panel the lyre, trumpet and laurel wreath are symbols of poetry. Pastoral poetry in panel three is symbolised by the trumpet, shepherd's crook and panpipe, the latter evoking the mythical god 'Pan' who appears as half man-half goat in the satyr mask set into the lunette fan at the back of the table. The fourth and last panel see emblems of love and learning with the torch, bow and arrows.

11 • MY MARQUETRY EDUCATION

These seductive images are, I believe, a mixture of mythical stories and factual events, hinting at the powerful presence of the men who changed the world, or as Jenny Uglow's title suggests — 'The friends who made the future'.

However, it is not until we look at the five ivory heads that we see a distinct connection with the achievements of the Lunar Men and their inspirational discoveries and inventions.

The central head, in Figure 11.9, represents Apollo, the all-embracing mythical God, with his lyre. On either side of Apollo, working from left to right we have the four heads shown in Figure 11.10.

Figure 11.9*
The central ivory head, with the lyre depicting poetry.

'Air' is represented by a bird in flight, followed by 'Earth', a figure wearing the mural crown, a symbol representing notable achievements of outstanding significance. To the right is 'Water' (a fish) and far right 'Fire' showing Vulcan holding a fork.

Figure 11.10* Four ivory heads depicting from left to right: Air, Earth, Water and Fire.

These four profiles — Air, Earth, Water and Fire — represent the ancient elements, the very elements that formed the basis for the inventions and productions that emerged from the scientific and industrial activities of the Lunar Men. Earth, provided the clay for Josiah Wedgwood to produce his ceramics, and fire to heat his kilns. Air and fire allowed Joseph Priestley to experiment and discover oxygen (called 'phlogiston' and also a nickname he carried to his grave) as well as the gases nitrogen and hydrogen with assistance from James Keir. Water and fire combined to produce the steam, helping James Watt to experiment towards the first efficient steam-driven engine. And finally, all four elements allowed Matthew Boulton to manufacture his ormolu and brass mounts and coins for the Royal Mint, since each needed the base mineral extracts from the earth, and fire, air and water to forge the end products.

The final element on the table is the lunette fan (Figure 11.11). I believe the image was deliberately intended to represent the moon, and I now have

*Reproduced by kind permission of the private collector

Figure 11.11* Lunette fan and satyr mask of the mythical god Pan

firm evidence to support this. How provocative of the designer to show 'Pan' (or perhaps a Lunar Man) emerging from darkness into the light, from ignorance to enlightenment. Dare I suggest an 'artistic scenario' was selectively included here!

The stunning reproduction of the marquetry work in Figure 11.7 shows the dye 'madder' (*Rubia tinctorum*) used for the red swags. Burgundy dye 'campeachy' (*Haematoxylum campechianum*) was used to depict the four anthemions above the red swags, proving that nature is perfectly replicated, because anthemions (honeysuckle as we know them) have burgundy fronds prior to their opening into flower.

The most compelling evidence however, from this scientific exercise is the 'lack of dye' to the lunette fan, whereas the circular fans repeated around the circumference were dyed pinkish/orange. The lunette fan, as we know, is constructed from nature's whitest wood, holly (*Ilex aquifolium*), confirming the deliberate intent to represent the moon. The small samples of dye results I have given here illustrate the lengths Chippendale went to precisely reproduce each object. It also speaks volumes for the reliability of Dr Heinrich Piening's dye analysis performed in 2008.

Further evidence in support of my hypothesis linking the pier table and the Lunar Men comes from a paper written by Eric Robinson titled 'Matthew Boulton and the Art of Parliamentary Lobbying' (*The Historical Journal* vii, 2 (1964), pp. 209–29). Watt's Fire-Engine Act of 1775 recalls Mathew Boulton approaching MPs to ease the act through parliament. One of the members of parliament was Edward Lascelles, then MP for Scarborough. Clearly the Lunar Men were known by the Lascelles family. Watt's Fire-Engine Bill received Royal Assent on 22 May 1775. The Lunar Society was formally established between February and May 1775, and Chippendale delivered this pier table and the silver-gilded wall furniture to Harewood on 1 December in the same year.

*Reproduced by kind permission of the private collector

11 • MY MARQUETRY EDUCATION

As a practising marqueteur, I consider the flawless marquetry of the pier table to be Chippendale's and England's finest. It is my hope that by disclosing my hypothesis, further evidence and thoughts will emerge regarding the outline plans for the decoration of the Yellow Drawing Room.

Here in 2022, twelve years since I wrote this article, I am even more convinced that my discovery regarding the link with the Lunar Men and Chippendale's masterful table is correct.

Chippendale was so specific about every stage of his process that every element of his work was 'stage managed' to become 'his brand'. Carvings on mahogany furniture and his selection of dyed colours in his marquetry work were so specifically chosen to match the precise meaning behind each artistic image, that they also became 'his brand'.

Choosing a white veneer to depict the moon on the Lunar Table was never an accident; he wanted the world to know about the Lunar Men's revolutionary contribution to our country, and he used his final and finest furniture creation to relay that story.

Through that we witness the genius of a great man.

As I close this book here in 2022, I would never have dreamt as an 83-year-old senior citizen, I would identify my Chippendale marquetry team, made up of men who, over the past thirty years, have given me the greatest marquetry masterclass I could hope for. I have been studying, emulating and writing about their exceptional talents, with veneers, dyes, inlaying, two-part fretsawing, sandshading, engraving and their countless construction techniques. To that, I can now add their earlier contributory talents under their previous employer.

These finds have also allowed me to answer questions I raised in my first book (*Chippendale's classic Marquetry Revealed*), which as you have seen, have been proved to be correct. I am so lucky to have been able to use the hands-on marquetry skills I am blessed with, allowing me to make ground-breaking discoveries surrounding and linking five multi-national, multi-skilled giants of the eighteenth century, namely:

Name	*Profession*	*Nationality*
Thomas Chippendale	Furniture designer	British
Pierre Langlois	Furniture designer	British
[John] Zurn	Inlayer	German
J.M. Dutton	Engraver/inlayer	British
Dominique Jean	Metal founder	French

However, I cannot close without paying tribute once again to the unique skills which were initially planted by my dear late Uncle and mentor, Tommy Limmer, who departed this earth twenty-three years ago, yet sadly never witnessed the amazing advancement gained purely from the teachings he forged into my craving hands, hungry mind, and eager heart. All of which reshaped the arc of my life forever.

Tommy Limmer (right), seen here with the author, in 1994 at the Leeds Marquetry Group's exhibition held at the Leeds Industrial Museum at Armley Mills

CHAPTER TWELVE

BIBLIOGRAPHY

Beard, Geoffrey & Gilbert, Christopher (1986) *Dictionary of English Furniture Makers 1660–1840*, London: Furniture History Society and W. S. Maney & Son

BIFMO (British and Irish Furniture Makers Online) – the Furniture History Society's free online database and research resource: www.furniturehistorysociety.org/bifmo

Chippendale, Thomas (1754 [1st Edition]; 1755 [2nd Edition]; 1762 [3rd Edition]), *The Gentleman and Cabinet-maker's Director: Being a Large Collection of Designs of Household Furniture in the Gothic, Chinese and Modern Taste*, London: T. Chippendale

Gilbert, Christopher (1978) *The Life and Work of Thomas Chippendale*, New York: Tabard Press

Gilbert, Christopher (1996) *Pictorial Dictionary of Marked London Furniture 1700–1840*, London: Routledge

Metcalfe, Jack (2009) 'A Chippendale Tribute to the Lunar Society', *The Furniture History Society Newsletter* No. 176, November 2009, pp.1–5

Metcalfe, Jack (2018) *Chippendale's classic Marquetry Revealed*, Leeds: J. Metcalfe

Metcalfe, Jack (2021) *The Warrington Chest 1888* (Chapter 4, 'Marquetry'), Tools and Trade History Society (TATHS)

Metcalfe, Jack & Apps, John (2003) *The Marquetry Course*, London: Batsford

Metcalfe, Jack & Apps, John (2020) *The classic Marquetry Course* (2nd Edition), Leeds: J. Metcalfe

Metcalfe, Jack (2020) trans. Hans Michaelsen *Die Kunst des Holzfärbens* (The art of Wood Dyeing – Synthetic Dyestuffs versus historical Wood Stains).

Thornton, Peter and Rieder, William (1971–2) 'Pierre Langlois, ébéniste', Parts 1–5, *Connoisseur*, Vol. 178 (Dec 1971), pp. 283–88; Vol. 179 (Feb–Apr 1972), pp. 105–12, 176–87, 257–65; Vol. 180 (May 1972), pp. 30–35.

Uglow, Jenny (2002) *The Lunar Men: the friends who made the future*, London: Faber & Faber

Wood, Lucy (1994) *Catalogue of Commodes*, London: HMSO Publications

Wood, Lucy (2014) 'New light on Pierre Langlois (1718–1767)', *The Furniture History Society Newsletter* No. 196, November 2014, pp.1–7

INDEX

Apps, John 58
arrow motif 10, 17, 40, 64
Aske Hall commode 19–21, 27–8, 54–5

Banks, Simon 19
Barstow, Philippa 60
bellflower motif 3, 6, 18, 21, 22, 39
Boulle, André-Charles 33
Boulton, Matthew 64, 65, 66
bow and arrows motif 10, 17, 40, 64
Bowett, Adam 20, 54
brasswork 9, 11, 12, 26, 27, 31, 35, 37, 38, 41, 42, 46, 55

Chazen Museum of Art, Madison, Wisconsin (Langlois commode) 15–16
Chippendale Tercentenary Exhibition 2018 20, 54
Chippendale, Thomas (the Elder)
   collaboration with P. Langlois and D. Jean 26–8, 29, 44, 46–7, 48
   Director, The Gentleman & Cabinet Maker's 2, 3–6, 7, 13–14, 33, 39–40, 55–6
   furniture commissions
      Aske Hall commode 19–21, 27–8, 54–5
      Diana & Minerva commode (Harewood House) 39, 50–3, 59–60, 62
      Lady Winn's commode (Nostell Priory) 20, 54–5
      library writing table (Harewood House) 48–50
      'Lunar' table (Harewood House) 40, 62–7
      mahogany commode (Nostell Priory) 26, 31, 37, 38
      pier tables (replicas) 58, 60–2

influence on Langlois 7, 13, 55–6
marquetry motifs 3–6, 39–40, 64–7
marquetry techniques 44–5, 48–53
use of dyed veneers 30, 66–7
Chippendale, Thomas (the Younger) 47
Clements, Ted 19
Computer Numerical Control (CNC) 55–6

Dahlström, Carl Petter 7
Darwin, Erasmus 63
Day, Thomas 63
Diana & Minerva commode (Harewood House) 39, 50–3, 59–60, 62
Dingwall, Patrick 19
Director, The Gentleman & Cabinet Maker's 2, 3–6, 7, 13–14, 33, 39–40, 55–6
Dundas, Mark 19, 27
Dundas, Sir Lawrence 28
Dutton, H. or [J.] M. 41–2, 46, 47, 53, 59, 67
dyeing 29–30, 66, 67
dye tests 2, 13, 31

engraving 29, 34, 36, 37, 38, 52–3, 61, 67

fan motif 3, 57, 60, 64, 65–6
fretsaw 23–5, 29, 33, 37, 44–6, 48–52, 57, 60
   treadle fretsaw 25, 45, 50
   two-part fretsawing 33, 45, 50, 57, 67
Furlohg, Christopher 7, 25, 53
Furniture History Society 27, 62

Index

Getty Museum, Los Angeles (Oeben toilette table) 11–13
Gilbert, Christopher 26, 31, 42

harwood 61, 62
Harewood House, Yorkshire 57
    Diana & Minerva commode 39, 50–3, 59–60, 62
    library writing table 48–50
    'Lunar' table 40, 62–7
    pier tables (replicas) 58, 60–2
Haupt, Georg 7, 25, 53
Huber, Jurgen 1

Jean, Dominique 13, 26, 27, 35, 37, 38, 42, 46, 47, 55, 67

Keir, James 63, 65

Lady Winn's commode (Nostell Priory) 20, 54–5
Lange, Thomas 1, 27, 31, 42
Langlois, Daniel (son of Pierre) 46–7
Langlois, Pierre 1, 2,
    biography 7
    brasswork 9, 26–7, 31, 35, 37, 38, 41, 42, 46, 55
    collaboration with Chippendale 26–8, 46–7
    commodes
        Aske Hall commode 19–21, 27–8, 54–5
        Chazen Museum of Art, Madison, USA 15–16
        Metropolitan Museum, NY 13–18, 28, 46, 55
        'Philips' commodes 31–6, 38, 46
        The Vyne, Hampshire) 42–3
    marquetry motifs 3–6, 9, 10, 13, 21–22, 33–40
    marquetry techniques 23–5
    pier table (Temple Newsam House) 21–2
    workshop 46–7
Langlois, Tracey (wife of Pierre) 27, 46–7

Lascelles family of Harewood House 64, 66
Limmer, Tommy ('Uncle Tommy') 57–8
Lomax, James 20, 54
Long, Malcolm 61
'Lunar' table (Harewood House) 40, 62–7

Martin, Elias 24–5, 53
Metropolitan Museum, New York
    Langlois commodes 13–18, 28, 46, 55
    Oeben toilette table 9–11
modifiers 29
mordants 29

Newby Hall, Yorkshire 61–2
Nostell Priory, Yorkshire
    games table 40, 48
    Lady Winn's commode 20, 54–5
    mahogany commode 26, 31, 37, 38

Oeben, Jean-François 7–13, 14, 33

pH (power of Hydrogen) 29–30
Piening, Heinrich 1, 12, 30, 31, 60, 66
Pompadour, Madame de 10
Priestley, Joseph 63, 65

quiver motif 10, 40, 64

Residenz Museum, Munich (Oeben toilette table) 98–9
ribbon motif 3, 13, 17, 18, 22, 38, 39–40
Ronald Phillips Ltd, Mayfair, London 1, 27, 31, 35, 42
Roubo, André Jacob 23
Russell, John 1, 27, 35

sandshading 3, 34, 36, 37, 57, 67
St Martin's Lane, London 2, 7, 29, 46
swag motif 3, 6, 18, 21, 22, 39, 66

71

Temple Newsam House, Leeds 21–2, 30
The Vyne, Hampshire (Langlois commodes) 42–3
torch motif 10, 40, 64
Tottenham Court Road, London 1, 2, 4, 7, 27, 46, 47, 52
treadle fretsaw 25, 45, 50

UV-VIS Spectronomy 2, 12, 13, 30, 60

veneers 33–4, 36, 44, 45, 48–51, 67
   dyeing 29–30

Watt, James 63, 64, 65, 66
Wedgwood, Josiah 63, 65
Wood, Lucy 7, 27–8, 47, 54

Zurn, [J?] 42, 44, 46, 47, 59, 67

www.ingramcontent.com/pod-product-compliance
Lightning Source LLC
Chambersburg PA
CBHW042258280426
43661CB00097BA/1186